The Holocaust

The Holocaust

The Nazi Destruction of Europe's Jews

Gerhard Schoenberner

Translated from the German by Susan Sweet
With a new introduction by Allan Gould

Hurtig Publishers
Edmonton

Hurtig Publishers Ltd.
10560 – 105 Street
Edmonton, Alberta
Canada T5H 2W7

Originally published in German as *Der Gelbe Stern*
Copyright © 1960 Gerhard Schoenberner

Revised and enlarged edition
Copyright © 1969 Gerhard Schoenberner

English translation
Copyright © 1969 Transworld Publishers Ltd.

Introduction by Allan Gould
Copyright © 1985 Allan Gould

Corgi edition published 1969
Hurtig Publishers reprint published 1985, with permission

Printed and bound in Canada
by Tri-graphic Printing (Ottawa) Limited

Publisher's Note

With so many daily headlines reminding us of the terrible events of the past, one might think that the reprinting of a book like this one would not be necessary. The search for war criminals, the commemorations of the fortieth anniversary of the liberation of the Nazi death camps, the recent reunions of survivors in Israel, New York and Ottawa, the furore over President Reagan's visit to a German military cemetery where soldiers of the *Wehrmacht* and SS were buried—it would seem quite inconceivable that the murder of six million Jews might be the subject of venomous debate.

But recently there have been numerous other headlines showing a dangerous, ugly side of our society, and its hateful, distorted lies, as painfully propagated during the trials of Ernst Zundel in Toronto and James Keegstra in Red Deer, Alberta, and by the Aryan Nations of Idaho and The Institute for Historical Review in California. Incredibly, today, in the mid 1980s, we witness vile attempts by neo-Nazis and anti-Semites to deny that the Holocaust ever took place.

This is why Hurtig Publishers has chosen to republish *The Yellow Star* with a new introduction at this time. The evil, fanatical slanders and libels cannot be ignored, and what better way to respond than through this remarkable collection of documents and photographs from the dozen years of horror of the Third Reich? The words are primarily those of the killers, as are the two hundred photographs.

Nothing can open the minds and hearts of those who are determined to maliciously corrupt history. But for men and women of good will, who overwhelmingly outnumber the twisted haters, this book can be a source of insight, and awareness, combined with pain—and yet, hope as well: hope that the truth can make us freer of evil, that knowledge of such deeds can strengthen our resolve never to let them happen again.

Mel Hurtig

Contents

An Introduction for the Mid-1980s

This book, with its two hundred photographs and dozens of documents, giving evidence of the most enormous crime against humanity in world history, should need no introduction. But, alas, the times in which we live demand a number of them. Gerhard Schoenberner's preface, a devastating statement by a German about the Holocaust and its meaning, was written in 1960, barely fifteen years after the death camps of the murderers were forced to stop their devastation. And while it is powerful and poetic, the events since that early date cry out for further comment, since only four decades after the end of Nazi barbarism, fascists and anti-Semites around the world still dare to deny the proven and documented historical facts, and insult the surviving victims, without fear of being prosecuted effectively by the courts, or repudiated by public opinion.

Denial is, of course, a most human response. We all deny things, often many times a day. Denial can be touchingly hopeful, as we all know from the stories of men and women who refuse to give in to a seemingly hopeless situation. In the case of the Jews who were caught up in the maelstrom of destruction and slaughter which we now label The Holocaust, their denial was, in hindsight, poignantly and pathetically optimistic. I have spoken with survivors who recall saying to themselves, upon their arrival at Auschwitz, stumbling from the hideously overcrowded trains, jostled by the milling throngs, the air acrid with smoke, stench, and death, ''This *can't* be as bad as it looks; this is the middle of the twentieth century, and these soldiers are the children of the most civilized nation in Europe!''

The seeming explosion of Holocaust denial, on the other hand, is neither human nor humane. It is obviously a conscious attempt by Nazi and neo-Nazi apologists to cover up the worst excesses of National Socialism, and thus rehabilitate the murderers of over ten million civilians during the dozen years of power of the Third Reich.

There are some aspects of denying the Holocaust which are understandable and even forgivable, paralleling the way in which most of us live from day to day, attempting to ignore the precipice of nuclear devastation upon which we all stand. We speak of concentration camps (when we speak of them at all), rather than of *death* camps, which so many of them were, or eventually became, by the end of the war. We say ''forced labour,'' as if the more truthful phrase ''slave labour'' would catch in our throats. And most upsetting—even though it is done by nearly all historians and commentators, even the surviving victims—we talk of the ''extermination'' of Jews, rather than their killing, or their murder. The use of this word, in fact, is to use the language of the Nazis, who spoke of their powerless arch enemies as lice, vermin, rats, only fit to be poisoned or gassed.

But this debasement and misuse of language, unfortunate as it is, is relatively harmless, compared with the lies and denials of the so-called ''revisionists.'' The deniers of the Holocaust, with all their pseudo-scientific blatherings, are falsifiers, out to refuse the reality of an historical event.

One would gladly ignore them. But the last quarter-century has seen a surge of these people, across Europe and North America, spreading their outrageous lies around the world. The American historian, and author of *The War Against the Jews 1933–1945*, Lucy S. Dawidowicz, put it concisely: ''... would Americans give a respectful hearing to someone who insisted that slavery had never existed in the United States, that blacks invented the story in order to get preferential treatment and federal aid, or that blacks had actually owned all the plantations? Somehow one doubts it.''

In a superb essay in *Commentary* magazine, ''Lies About the Holocaust'' (December, 1980), the same historian tracked down the ''swarm of Nazi apologists, cranks and anti-Semites'' who have been working on denying the Holocaust since the early 1960s. Each has proven himself to be more fascistic than academic. Surprisingly, some American historical societies have been generous to the point of even reviewing some of these pseudo-scientific works, which tend to deny that Hitler was responsible for the ''final solution,'' that gas chambers ever existed, or that they were used for murdering human beings. Dawidowicz then quotes the final paragraph from a declaration of nearly three dozen prominent French historians, reacting to those slanders. It is worth reprinting here:

> Everyone is free to interpret a phenomenon like the Hitlerite genocide according to his own philosophy. Everyone is free to compare it with other enterprises of murder committed earlier, at the same time, later. Everyone is free to offer such or such kind of explanation; everyone is free, to the limit, to imagine or to dream that these monstrous deeds did not take place. Unfortunately, they did take place and no one can deny their existence without committing an outrage on the truth. It is not necessary to ask how technically such a mass murder was possible. It was technically possible, seeing that it took place. That is the required point of departure of every historical inquiry on this subject. This truth it behooves us to remember in simple terms: there is not and there cannot be a debate about the existence of the gas chambers.

Tragically, if not surprisingly, these obscene debates continue. The Zundel case in Toronto, Canada, in 1985, is but the most recent example of this so-called revisionism. Ernst Zundel has steadily become one of the world's largest publishers and exporters of anti-Jewish hate-literature over the previous decade. It was only after a survivor of the Holocaust which he was continually questioning laid a private charge against the propagandist, that he was eventually tried. Unfortunately, it was under a rarely used and vague Canadian law (Section 177 of the Criminal Code) which provides that "every one who willfully publishes a statement, tale or news that he knows is false and that causes or is likely to cause injury or mischief to a public interest is guilty of an indictable offence and is liable to imprisonment for two years."

The two charges against Zundel were directed against two of his pamphlets, one of which spouted the century-old canard that there is an international conspiracy of Jews, Freemasons, bankers, and communists to rule the world. The other was the now-notorious attack on the veracity of the Holocaust, claiming that the event was a hoax, used by the State of Israel to obtain reparations from Germany after the Second World War.

If the use of the law against the racist publisher was absurd (it was developed in England many centuries ago, to protect King Edward I and his noblemen from slanderous rumours), the case itself quickly became a grotesque parody of reality and decency: Zundel's lawyer attempted to prove his client's words true by putting the Holocaust *itself* on trial. In other words, not unlike the "second rape" of sexual assault victims by an unfeeling court, many survivors of the period were forced to "prove" that they *had* been ghettoized, starved, worked to exhaustion, their families murdered.

Margaret Laurence, one of Canada's finest novelists, wrote to the Toronto newspapers at the time: "How many times must the victims of the Nazi brutality (not the whole German people throughout history, for God's sake), humiliated and tortured in their lives, be humiliated again through this man's words? Are the innocent dead expected to die again and again? O Canada, where are the cries of public outrage and the concern for justice and humanity?"

Less painful, but no less insulting and obnoxious, was the badgering of such world-renowned and respected scholars as Raul Hilberg, a professor at the University of Vermont and the author of the seminal work, *The Destruction of the European Jews*, based entirely on the Nazis' own documentation.

But most unsettling of all was the parade of Jew-haters, convicted felons, and dubious heroes of the "revisionist" movement, who came to speak on behalf of the accused, among them Ditlieb Felderer, previously convicted in Sweden for spreading racial hatred, and Dr. Robert Faurisson, who had been successfully prosecuted three times in France for libel, racial defamation, and falsifying the history of the Holocaust.

In the prosecution's closing address, the Crown attorney captured the *raison d'être* of the "revisionists" perfectly: "What is the major stumbling block to the rehabilitation of the Nazis?" he asked the jury. "I'd suggest it is the Holocaust. So long as the greatest inhumanity man has ever done to man exists as a historically accepted fact in the minds of men, the Nazis can never be rehabilitated. He must get rid of it. So he publishes a pamphlet replete with lies."

The judge and jury agreed, with the former describing Zundel as "a neo-Nazi propagandist," and sentencing him to a 15-month jail sentence. Zundel, the judge declared, "has slandered the memory of innocent murdered human beings." Understandably, many Canadian lawyers, while sympathetic toward the anguish of the targets of Zundel's attacks and outraged by Zundel's lies, question the legality of the laws, and the result of the massive press coverage which the propagandist received. ("It cost me $40,000 in lost work," stated the man upon his conviction, "but I got $1 million worth of publicity for my cause. It was well worth it".)

Newspaper headlines across Canada screamed that "Zundel won the propaganda war," and commentators moaned that there must surely be a more effective way to undermine the purveyors of hate than by disseminating their message for them. The most thoughtful criticism of the Zundel case was made by George Bain, one of the country's most respected journalists and teachers:

> *What has been proved by Ernst Zundel's conviction? That the Holocaust really happened? That Ernst Zundel lied? But of course it happened. The camps are there . . . we have talked to survivors. There are tens of thousands of witnesses to the history of the time and thousands of well-researched and written accounts. The writings of Zundel and others like him amount to very little against that large body of testimony, which cannot be wiped out. But now we have an official truth, a court decision to be cited—and that can. If the decision of the recent court was that Zundel's dismissal of the Holocaust as a fraud was false, what would be the effect of a successful appeal? That it was true? That the Holocaust didn't happen?*

Ironically enough, the neo-Nazi was found *not* guilty of printing that *second* pamphlet, which argued that Jews and others were working together to rule the world. Zundel, then, was acquitted for writing the same nonsense that James Keegstra, who had appeared as an "expert witness" at Zundel's trial, was about to go on trial for *teaching*.

The Keegstra case, which began only days after Zundel's concluded, in early 1985, is in some ways even more grotesque than the earlier one: whereas Zundel denied the murder of millions of Jews, Keegstra taught his high school students for many years the same forgeries and slanders which the Nazis had used to incite their followers to *kill* the Jews! In other words, the pamphlet for which Zundel was *acquitted* for publishing was part of the material from which Keegstra purportedly incited hatred in his students.

The portion of the Canadian Criminal Code used to prosecute James Keegstra was barely more promising than that used against the "revisionist" publisher Zundel: Section 281.2 calls for charges against anyone who "by communicating statements, other than in private conversation, wilfully promotes hatred against an identifiable group."

For a number of weeks, over two dozen of Keegstra's former students came forth and read to the court from their notebooks: that the world would have been better if Hitler had won the war; that the Talmud allows Jews to steal from Gentiles; that "Zionist Jews" control the world's press and financial institutions, and manipulate the governments of the United States, Soviet Union, France and China; and so on, ad nauseum.

What was so troubling about the Keegstra trial was that much of the man's teachings was drawn from an ancient forgery best known as "The Protocols of the Elders of Zion." British scholar Norman Cohn, in his 1967 study *(Warrant for Genocide, The Myth of the Jewish World-Conspiracy and the Protocols of the Elders of Zion)*, traces the warped belief back to feudal France, threatened by the French Revolution, shows how it was used to provoke pogroms in Czarist Russia, in order to calm down social unrest, swept the globe in the 1920s, and, during the 1930s and 1940s, provided the ideology for the near-total destruction of the Jews of Europe. Even more dreadful is the fact that various versions of the Protocols continue to be printed—in millions of copies—in South America and in a number of Arab countries, continuing its creation of collective psychopathology, as it did with James Keegstra. The fact that the schoolteacher was convicted and fined $5,000 for wilfully promoting hatred against Jews—"he is akin to a drug addict pushing drugs" declared the judge—will do little to stop the disease from spreading.

Jew-haters will probably always be among us, and trials against libelers and slanderers will more than likely continue to come to court. A major victory occurred in Los Angeles in August, 1985, when Melvin Mermelstein, whose family had been murdered in Nazi death camps, won $90,000 and an apology from the anti-Semitic Liberty Lobby of Washington, D.C., and Willis Carto, of the California-based Institute for Historical Review, for their Holocaust denial. The defendants also agreed to accept a 1981 court ruling that said the murder of Jews at Auschwitz was an indisputable fact. But men and women of good will are surely going to continue to question whether or not the courts are appropriate places to combat "revisionism." It is a sad fact that existing laws are not sufficient to deal with these criminals, much as they proved to be insufficient to deal with the murderers, who had committed state-organized mass crimes.

In the last analysis, the only hope against the vicious Holocaust denial of the "revisionists" is in education. And education for parents as well; surely the most frightening aspect of the Keegstra case is *not* that one man could swallow a lunatic belief in a world conspiracy, but that so many parents over so many years could read the hate-filled notes and essays of their children, and not be moved to revulsion and action against the perpetrator. Yet textbooks used across North America continue to be shamefully lacking in any references to the Nazi treatment of minorities, whether they were the physically and mentally disabled, political opponents, Slavs, gypsies, homosexuals, prisoners of war, or Jews.

The physical annihilation of nearly six million men, women and children of Jewish origin was unique, and its radical evil should make us all justifiably uncomfortable. While there have been horrendous massacres throughout history which saw one people destroy another, never before have we seen the actual murders as a fulfillment of an ideology; never before, mass murder as an end in itself, and not merely a means to an end. The astonishing fact that, countless times between 1942–1945, trains that were desperately needed to provide munitions for German soldiers on the front were diverted to transport Jews to their deaths, must make us all long to disbelieve such self-destructive actions. But it is hardly the fact that the Nazi murderers failed to act in their own self-interest which should horrify us; it is the unthinkable cruelty and unimaginable dimension of the mass-killings which we must confront. And we must believe it, because it happened. The general awareness of the Holocaust has made it a litmus test for human rights and decency: surely it was knowledge of the Nazi destruction of European Jews which moved so many Americans and Canadians to open their doors to the Boat People in the 1970s, and to send money and food to the starving Ethiopians in the mid-1980s.

The Holocaust, because of its terrible uniqueness, its towering numbers of tortured and dead, its dreadful implications of just how thin a veneer our civilization truly is, is almost impossible to confront, even by people open to its awful lessons. That is why this book is being reprinted. The documents, the painful photographs, might well sink in where a lengthy novel, history, or autobiography cannot. Yet even this is optimistic. Elie Wiesel, who has done more than any other survivor to raise the world's consciousness to what it did, or allowed to be done, to the Jewish people, recently wrote:

No, I do not understand. And if I write, it is to warn the reader that he will not understand either. "You will not understand, you will never understand," were the words heard everywhere during the reign of night. I can only echo them. You, who never lived under a sky of blood, will never know what it was like. Even if you read all the books ever written, even if you listen to all the testimonies ever given, you will remain on this side of the wall, you will view the agony and death of a people from afar, through a screen of memory that is not your own.

One cannot question the truth of Wiesel's words, any more than one can question the crimes of the Nazis and the deadly silence of the rest of the world in those years. But we can read books like this one, look into the faces of the doomed and their destroyers in the photographs, and vow to make our own lives, and those of our loved ones, be filled with tolerance for others, and action against injustice, wherever it occurs.

Allan Gould
Toronto, Canada
August 1985

Introduction to Previous Edition

Shops are being looted and synagogues are burning. On the outskirts of Lodz, hundreds of sledges are drawn through the snow into the ghetto. An old man, supported by his son, totters to the deportation train. In a Russian village, the condemned are gathered together in a sad open-air mass meeting. In Amsterdam a small boy waits at the registration point, his little wooden horse beside him. And a uniformed doctor stands on the platform in Auschwitz, selecting fellow creatures for the gas chamber.

What does all this mean?

They called it "resettlement" when they transported people to the death camp, said "confiscation" as they robbed their victims of their last possessions, and spoke of "special treatment" when they meant murder.

What is shown in this book is Germany's own act. It happened through us, even if we did not do it ourselves. We condoned it: it concerns us. That is why we stand embarrassed before it, and would prefer not to know about it.

The persecution of Jews was only one crime—the most terrible—among countless others committed by the Nazis. But it provides a particularly clear example of the anti-human nature of Nazi ideology and its criminal character when put into practice. The wholesale murder of millions of innocent people was no perversion of National Socialism, but the logical application of its inherent principles.

Many books have been written on the phenomenon of anti-Semitism and on the gas-chamber regime that was its dreadful realisation. This book attempts to tell in pictures the story of the persecution of Jews by the Third Reich. It is a book of the dead. All the people shown here, unless exceptionally good fortune saved them, were murdered. Only their persecutors, unless exceptional misfortune overtook them, are still alive.

In this book, what was in fact an endless process of mounting suffering is collected into dramatic form. The years of humiliation, starvation, terror and death cannot be invoked by any photograph. They cannot be expressed in visual terms. The photographs can only convey some idea of what took place. They can only attempt to portray the experience of living and dying as suffered by others. They cannot make us see and feel it ourselves.

Can these photographs from the dark past still reach us in the bustle of our hastily normalised life? Are they not now almost a lie, appearing before us as they do today, a refined version of real life, without its filth, without the blood and without the screams of terror? Our imagination must add that missing atmosphere. We must imagine the air poisoned by brutality and horror. We must imagine the heavy tread of boots on the pavement and the arrogant voices of the conquerors, shouting orders in German and behaving like wild beasts because they have been taught that their victims are less than human. We do not hear the rattle of gunshots and the strangled sobs of the children as they hide their faces in their mothers' skirts. We do not smell the choking stench drifting across the camp from the ovens where human beings burn. We do not hear the surrealist counterpoint of the gay operetta music accompanying the prisoners as they march out to work in the morning and the death transports as they go to the gas chambers.

The biblical prophesies of Judgment Day and the fearful visions of Kafka became reality. The monsters of Hieronymus Bosch rose up in human form. They did not have tusks or hooves or the faces of toads. They were clean-shaven, wore their hair neatly parted and were good family men. They travelled by car and aeroplane, and killed by teleprinter and chemical poisons. Dante's Inferno was established in the modern world.

In the same way as Nazi propaganda seemed credible by the very enormity of its untruth, because nobody thought that lies of such a fantastic order would be told, Nazi crimes were so inconceivable that their authors could rest assured in the knowledge that the German people would never believe the truth about them, dismissing it as foreign propaganda.

5

I remember when I saw the Auschwitz Museum for the first time: the store-rooms stacked to the ceiling with clothes and shoes; the wagon-loads of women's hair, tooth-brushes, spectacles, artificial limbs and suitcases displayed behind great glass windows. I found myself then desperately hoping that this was only a bad dream; that the astronomical figures given to us by our guide were based on miscalculations; that it was an optical illusion that made the overwhelming mountains of evidence—those mute, damning witnesses—seem to be heaped up to such a dreadful height. Yet I knew that this storehouse held only an infinitesimal part of the victims' personal belongings, the remnants that were left behind at the end of the war because they could no longer be carted away. And Auschwitz was only one of those death factories that killed and burned human beings, mechanically, by the wagon-load, in the same way that goods are turned out in other industries.

The illustrated papers have accustomed us to horror: fires, earthquakes, floods, a racing-car flung from the track, a man jumping to his death from a bridge. With tactless curiosity, the camera photographs into open coffins and the weeping faces of survivors. But nearly always it is natural disasters or individual misfortunes, witnessed more or less fortuitously by the reporters. The appalling thing about the photographs in this book is that here for the first time a State-planned crime, committed millionfold, is captured phase by phase in pictures. And most monstrous of all, it is the murderers who photographed themselves at work.

Imagine a professional thief and murderer asking a friend to photograph him as he selected his victims, lured them into the trap and killed them, and then to stick the photographs in an album as souvenirs. That is precisely what did happen. The photographs are almost without exception drawn from German sources. The majority were taken by official Press photographers for the regime and, to a lesser extent, by amateurs in German uniform.

Actual photograph albums were in fact compiled which recorded deportations and executions as if they were holidays spent at the seaside or in the mountains. In many historical archives we can still see these macabre travesties of the old family album. There are the official ones, which may have been intended for the archives of the Third Reich, and there are the private ones, which Hitler's warriors wanted to take home as souvenirs of the heroic deeds that earned them special rations of *Schnaps* and cigarettes and even medals, medals that are worn again today. It is always the small men—the henchmen, the slave-drivers and the killers—who are seen here. There are no photographs that adequately depict the activity of the top men—the theorists and organisers, the propagandists and chief shareholders of the racist delusion. They remained at their desks and did not show themselves in the places where their plans were carried out.

The photographs do not exaggerate. Had they been taken from the point of view of those being persecuted, depicting their own sufferings and the atrocities of their tormentors, a quite different picture would have emerged. Perhaps many people in Germany today would learn much if they could see the "master race" just once in the role in which a whole continent saw them and still remembers them.

The people shown here had no choice but to have their photographs taken. As they went to certain death, and often knowing that they must die, they saw the enemy's camera turned on them. Their eyes, as they look into the camera lens, meet ours as we look at these photographs some 40 years later and put us into the position of the murderers. There are looks of fearful expectation and hopeless despair, of utter terror and acceptance of their fate. Many of the faces have a distrustful, withdrawn expression. Others attempt a pitiful smile of fear to put the German master in a merciful mood. Yes, many fell on their knees and kissed the hands of the strangers in their uniforms with the death's-head insignia, begging for mercy. They still looked on them as human and thought they would be able to move them to pity. But the soldiers repeated to themselves that these were mere vermin, as they had been taught in their barracks and SS training centres, and carried out the orders of their superiors.

The source of the photographs gives them a twofold bias. In their delusion, the murderers felt themselves to be Siegfried overcoming the dragon. They saw themselves in the role of the hero and their defenceless victims as *Untermenschen*—subhuman. The photographs they took are an attempt to record these relative roles. The photographers took pains to photograph their subjects in as unfavourable a light as possible. They relied on the crude psychology that intimidated, tormented and exhausted people can easily repel the superficial observer. But they always also selected the physical characteristics that were, to their way of thinking, particularly unattractive and that came nearest to the distorted caricature of the Jew instilled by Nazi anti-Semitic propaganda.

It is moving to see how the truth, despite everything, comes through again and again in these photographs: how much human dignity the victims preserve in utmost degradation and helplessness. The vainly swaggering brutality and violence, on the other hand, become contemptible and vile in comparison. Be they round-faced little children or wasted old men, the thought that they were murdered brings them close to us, and convinces us of the right to live of every one of them. Whether the men in uniform have the hard, pinched faces of cruelty or the soft features of youth, in this situation and condemned by these acts, they stand before us as murderers.

On the other hand, the photographs attempt to conceal the savage and bloody character of the events, to prevent the slightest stirrings of human sympathy. That is why the pictures of life in the Warsaw Ghetto and of its destruction, and also the photographs that came out of the death camps, are, compared to what we know from official and private accounts and from secret film records, almost unreal in their stylisation. The reality was that much worse. Yet, in spite of this self-imposed censorship, there is much that does come through. It was thought proper for women to be forced to undress in front of the men of a firing squad bristling with weapons, that mothers should carry their babies with them into the gas chamber, and that children had to look on while their parents were butchered. The pictures in this book reveal what the murderers considered fit to be photographed.

The documentation is necessarily incomplete. A lot has been left out. Photographs of the manufacture of soap from the corpses of murdered people, of men whose bodies were mutilated by the SS doctors, of lampshades made from tattooed human skin, and scalps processed in the manner of head-hunters were deliberately not included in this collection. There are naturalistic details that are, at most, of pathological interest, and that do not contribute to the general understanding of this tragedy of mankind.

There is no record of the lives of those in hiding and the fugitives who languished for many months in lofts or cellars until they fell into the the hands of the Gestapo, often as a result of carelessness or denunciation. We only have the eye-witness accounts of a few survivors describing the heroism of those who risked their own lives to help the victims of persecution, and of those who organised resistance to the inhuman system.

There is little available photographic material on the wholesale executions of the Jewish population in the occupied areas of the Soviet Union. By 1941 a general ban was imposed on the photographing of executions. An attempt was also made to confiscate all the photographs already in existence because it was feared that they might fall into enemy hands through the soldiers who had been taken prisoner. The available photographs give only an inadequate idea of the bestial brutality and the immense scale of this slaughter of a whole section of the population. Also, the camera leads us no further than the threshold of the gas chamber. What happened there, when the great bunker doors were bolted, was seen only by the SS, who followed the progress of the slow suffocation through small observation windows, and by the unfortunate prisoners in the special squads who had to clear away the corpses of the murdered people and put them into the ovens.

This last station remains hidden from us, we are spared the sight. The act of dying, death itself, are withdrawn from our gaze. But we do see the endless procession of the deportees from Germany and all the occupied countries of Europe set out on its road of suffering that led, by way of registration and the reception camp, the ghetto and forced labour, to the last station—extermination. We see a procession of millions, on foot, in carts, in goods wagons and lorries on the road into the void. We see the people undress, we see the ovens into which they disappeared, and we see the clothes and shoes that they left behind.

The years pass. The barracks in Birkenau, once full to overflowing with human misery and suffering, stand empty and dilapidated. The pits in which men burned have been filled by the rain and have become little pools grown around with rushes. Only the pale grey colour of the earth reminds us whose ashes are scattered here. Of the gas chambers and crematoria, which were blown up, there remain only a few solitary broken concrete slabs, and twisted iron wire stretching rusty fingers to the sky. Between the barracks big bushes of wild roses flourish and bloom. The ground, once trod hard by many thousands of clogs and where no blade grew, has become a meadow of waving grass, mown every summer.

"Bury the past," demand those who have something to hide. "Do not sully Germany's name," cry those who besmirched it with their bloody hands. "Let bygones be bygones," the murderers advise us. And there are many people who thoughtlessly repeat their words. They forget that outside Germany there is a much sharper memory of those years and that the facts which here often still meet with stubborn silence or with incredulous surprise are common knowledge. Those who kept silent when it was time to speak out talk loudly of forgiving and forgetting. Even well-meaning people speak at the most of shame. But there remains a shared guilt which one cannot easily buy oneself out of, and which cannot be "made good". No-one can bring the dead back to life. What is done cannot be undone.

Belated moral condemnation and humane regret are not enough. The historical facts must be made known, the social causes that made them possible must be understood, and we must become aware of our own responsibility for what goes on around us. We do not escape the past by thrusting it to the back of our minds. Only if we come to terms with it and understand the lessons of those years, can we free ourselves of the legacy of Hitlerite barbarism. Policies are not pre-ordained by fate. They are made by people and people can change them.

In Hitler's Germany

Anti-Semitism was a fundamental part of Hitler's programme. Anti-Semitism was the magic formula which he used to explain all social ills and gain the support of the politically disorientated petty bourgeoisie. Anti-Semitism was the means by which he smashed the legal system, established the dictatorship and implicated the German people in his crimes.

On 30th January 1933, Hitler came to power. The suppression of all opposition began. The *Reichstag* Fire was followed by open terror. Communists and Social Democrats were the first victims. At the same time the persecution of the Jews was intensified. Chanting bands of stormtroopers forced judges to break off court proceedings; professors could no longer deliver their lectures; pedestrians were knocked down in the streets.

In reply to the shocked reports that appeared in the world Press, the Government redoubled the terror. As a "counter-measure against Jewish atrocity propaganda," they organised the first official boycott of all Jewish doctors, lawyers and businessmen. Stormtroopers were posted in front of shops and offices. Anybody who ignored the warnings risked being beaten up and publicly pilloried. The boycott was soon extended to all spheres of cultural life. There was no longer room in Germany for the poetry of Heine and Mendelssohn's music, the works of Sigmund Freud and Einstein's formulae, Liebermann's painting and Reinhardt's theatre.

The "cleansing" of Jewish authors from public libraries developed into a campaign against contemporary German literature and intellectual freedom in general. 250 playwrights, Jews and non-Jews, were banned. Among them were such well-known names as Thomas Mann, Heinrich Mann, Bertolt Brecht, Arnold Zweig, Anna Seghers, Hugo von Hofmannsthal, Franz Werfel, Erich Kaestner and Kurt Tucholsky. Once Nazi propaganda had succeeded in popularising the absurd theory that the Jews were to blame for everything, any undesirable trend of thought or any opposition at all had only to be described as being under Jewish influence to justify its elimination and the physical persecution of its supporters. In this sense, everyone who opposed Hitler was a Jew and, if he were not a Jew, then he was a "stooge of the Jews". Every violent measure, from the banning of democratic parties and free trade unions to the campaign against the League of Nations, was carried out under the slogan of anti-Semitism.

The wild terror that anticipated the law was followed by the laws that legitimised the terror. Jewish citizens were excluded from one profession after another. The Government accompanied all these measures with an ever-mounting anti-Jewish smear campaign. They accused their victims of the most preposterous crimes to justify their actions in the eyes of the population, and to prepare the ground psychologically for further, still worse measures. In the summer of 1935, on the instructions of the Nazi party, notices were displayed throughout Germany warning Jews against entering restaurants, public baths and whole localities. In this way the impression was given to the general public that it was the German people that was forcing the legislators to intervene. On 15th September, the *Reichstag* passed the anti-Semitic Nuremberg Laws, the Reich Citizenship Law, which reduced Jews to the status of second-class citizens, and the medieval Law for the Protection of German Blood, which forbade marriage between Jews and non-Jews. They laid the basis for a whole flood of decrees and new laws which robbed the Jews of their last remaining rights. In 1938 the persecution mounted to an open pogrom. Synagogues were set on fire, the people hounded and maltreated, their homes and shops destroyed or plundered. The Government organised a great racket out of the "Aryanisation" of Jewish property and the imposition of a "Reich fugitive" tax on all emigrants.

People whose families had been settled in Germany for hundreds of years went abroad. The misery of emigration began. Anybody who did not actually go overseas was still in danger.

On 30th January 1939, Hitler threatened that, in the event of war, which he had already prepared, all Jews in Europe would be exterminated.

A School Essay

Dear *Stuermer*,

Gauleiter Streicher has told us so much about the Jews that we absolutely hate them. At school we wrote an essay called "The Jews are our Misfortune". I should like you to print my essay.

The Jews are our Misfortune

Unfortunately, many people today still say, "God created the Jews too. That is why you must respect them also." We say, however, "Vermin are also animals, but we still destroy them." The Jew is a half-caste. He has inherited characteristics of Aryans, Asiatics, Negroes and Mongols. In a half-caste, the worst characteristics predominate. The only good thing about him is his white colour. The South Sea Islanders have a proverb that goes: "God made the white man and God made the black man. But the devil made the half-caste." Jesus once said to them, "God is not your father, but the devil." The Jews have a wicked book of laws. It is called the Talmud. The Jews look on us as animals as well and treat us accordingly. They use cunning tricks to take away our wealth. The Jews ruled in the court of Karl of Franconia. That is why Roman law was introduced. This did not suit the German peasants: it was not a law for the Roman townsman-farmers either, but a Jewish merchant law. The Jews are also certainly guilty of the murder of Karl of Franconia.

In Gelsenkirchen the Jew Grueneberg sold us rotten meat. His book of laws allows him to do that. The Jews have plotted revolts and incited war. They have led Russia into misery. In Germany they gave the Communist Party money and paid their thugs. We were at death's door. Then Adolf Hitler came. Now the Jews are abroad and stir up trouble against us. But we do not waver and we follow the *Fuehrer*. We do not buy anything from the Jew. Every penny we give them kills one of our own people.

Heil Hitler.

Erna Listing, Gelsenkirchen, Oswaldstr. 8   *Reader's letter to "Der Stuermer", January 1935*

. . . and a Conference

On 6th July 1938, after much introductory skirmishing, the highly publicised Evian Conference was called to order . . .

One after another the nations made clear their unwillingness to accept refugees. Since the business meetings were closed to the Press, they did not risk public exposure.

Australia, with vast, unpopulated areas, announced: "As we have no real racial problem, we are not desirous of importing one." New Zealand was unwilling to lift its restrictions. The British colonial empire, reported Sir John Shuckburgh, contained no territory suitable to the large-scale settlement of Jewish refugees. Canada wanted agricultural migrants and no others. The same was true of Colombia, Uruguay and Venezuela.

Peru was particularly opposed to the immigration of doctors and lawyers lest such an intellectual proletariat upset the unbridled power of its upper class. The Peruvian delegate pointedly remarked that the United States had given his country an example of "caution and wisdom" by its own immigration restrictions.

France, whose population already included two hundred thousand refugees and three million aliens, stressed that it had reached its saturation point.

Nicaragua, Honduras, Costa Rica and Panama issued a joint statement saying that they could accept no "traders or intellectuals". Argentina, with a population one-tenth that of the United States, reported that it had welcomed almost as many refugees as the United States and hence could not be counted on for large-scale immigration.

The Netherlands and Denmark reflected their traditional humanitarianism. Though Holland had already accepted twenty-five thousand Jewish refugees, it offered itself as a country of temporary sojourn. Denmark, so densely populated that its own citizens were forced to emigrate, had already taken in a disproportionately large number of German exiles. Within its narrow limits it would continue to do so.

And the United States, that nation at whose initiative the conference had convened, what would it offer? The answer was soon in coming. The United States, with its tradition of asylum, its vast land mass and its unlimited resources, agreed for the first time to accept its full, legal quota of 27,370 immigrants annually from Germany and Austria. That was the major American concession made at Evian.

Arthur D. Morse

The Nuremberg Laws

ART. 1 (1) A subject of the State is one who belongs to the protective union of the German *Reich* and has, therefore, specific obligations to the *Reich* . . .

ART. 2 (1) Only the subject of the State who is of German or related blood, and who shows through his behaviour that he is desirous and fit loyally to serve the German people and *Reich*, is a citizen of the *Reich* . . .

ART. 3 The *Reich* Minister of the Interior in conjunction with the Deputy to the *Fuehrer* will issue the legal and administrative decrees required for the implementation and amplification of this law.

The Reich Citizenship Law of 15th September 1935

ART. 1 (1) Marriages between Jews and citizens of German or related blood are forbidden. Marriages contracted in contravention of this law are invalid, even if they are contracted abroad in order to circumvent this law.

(2) Annulment proceedings can be initiated only by the Public Prosecutor.

ART. 2 Extramarital relations between Jews and citizens of German or related blood are forbidden . . .

ART. 5 (1) Anyone who contravenes the prohibition under ART. 1 will be punished by penal servitude . . .

(2) The man who contravenes ART. 2 will be punished by imprisonment or penal servitude.

ART. 6 The *Reich* Minister of the Interior in conjunction with the Deputy to the *Fuehrer* and the *Reich* Minister of Justice will issue the legal and administrative decrees required for the implementation and amplification of this law.

Law for the Protection of German Blood and German Honour of 15th September 1935

. . . and the Commentary

The National Socialist leadership of the State holds the unshakable conviction that it is acting in accordance with the Almighty Creator in attempting to express in the State and folkish system of the Third *Reich*, in so far as this is possible with the imperfect means at the disposal of man, the eternal iron laws of life and nature that govern and determine the destiny of both the individual and the whole. The legal and State system of the Third *Reich* must be made to conform once more to the laws of life, the natural laws that are eternally valid for the body, mind and soul of the German people. In the folkish and State reform of our time it is a matter of neither more nor less than the recognition and restoration of the organic order of life, in the deepest sense willed by God, in the life of the German people and State . . .

The Blood Protection Law deals with the segregation of Jewish and German blood from the biological point of view. The increasing decline in appreciation of the importance of the purity of blood that took place in the decade before the Revolution, and the resultant destruction of all folkish values, demonstrate the urgency of legislative intervention. As an acute danger threatened the German people from Jewry alone, the law aims primarily at the prevention of further mixing of blood with Jews . . .

No law passed since the National Socialist Revolution is such a complete departure from the mental attitude and the concept of the State of the past century as is the *Reich* Citizenship Law. To the precepts of equality of all men and basic unrestricted freedom of the individual vis-à-vis the State, National Socialism opposes here the harsh but necessary recognition of the natural inequality and differences between men. From the differences between races, peoples and men there follow inevitably differences in the rights and duties of individuals. This diversity, based on life and immutable natural laws, is carried into effect by the *Reich* Citizenship Law in the political, fundamental system of the German people.

Stuckart/Globke, Commentaries to the German Race Laws, 1936

The Night of the Broken Glass

Berlin No. 234 404 9.11.2355
To all Gestapo Stations and Gestapo District Stations
To Officer or Deputy

This teleprinter message is to be submitted without delay
1. At very short notice, *Aktionen* against Jews, especially against their synagogues, will take place throughout the whole of Germany. They are not to be hindered. In conjunction with the police, however, it is to be ensured that looting and other particular excesses can be prevented.
2. If important archive material is in synagogues, this is to be taken into safe keeping by an immediate measure.
3. Preparations are to be made for the arrest of about, 20,000–30,000 Jews in the *Reich*. Wealthy Jews in particular are to be selected. More detailed instructions will be issued in the course of this night.
4. Should, in the forthcoming *Aktionen*, Jews be found in possession of weapons, the most severe measures are to be taken. SS Reserves as well as the General SS can be mobilised in the total *Aktionen*. The direction of the *Aktionen* by the *Gestapo* is in any case to be ensured by appropriate measures.

Gestapo II Mueller
This teleprinter message is secret

SA of the NSDAP

Darmstadt, 11th November 1938

To SA Group Kurpfalz, Mannheim

The following order reached me at 3 o'clock on 10th November 1938. "On the order of the *Gruppenfuehrer*, all the Jewish synagogues within the 50th Brigade are to be blown up or set on fire immediately. Neighbouring houses occupied by Aryans are not to be damaged. The *Aktion* is to be carried out in civilian clothes. Rioting and plundering are to be prevented. Report of execution of orders to reach *Brigadefuehrer* or station by 8.30."

Der Fuehrer der Brigade 50 (Starkenburg)

SS-Sturm 10/25

Geldern, 14th November 1938

Re: Aktion against the Jews

The *Aktion* in the district of Geldern, as well as Xanten, was carried out exclusively by members of the *SS-Sturm* 10/25. The orders were issued by telephone by the *SS-Sturmbann* III/25 on 10.11.1938 at about 9.30 hours.

The first measure was the setting on fire of the synagogue in Geldern at about 4.0 a.m. By 9.0 a.m. this was burned down to the foundations. Some bibles in Hebrew characters were taken into safe keeping. Simultaneously the interior fittings of the synagogue in Xanten (a private house) were completely destroyed. There existed two Jewish shops in the *Sturm* district, the fittings and small stock of which were likewise completely destroyed.

The furnishings of the remainder of the Jews, former cattle-Jews and now earning their living by private means, were totally demolished and rendered unusable, the windows and windowpanes first having been broken in . . .

By about 11 hours all the male Jews from 15 to 70 years of age were arrested by the police and kept temporarily in the local guard-houses . . . The population took a passive attitude to the demonstrations . . . As there were no large shops, there were no cases of looting . . .

Der Fuehrer des SS-Sturms 10/25

Grunewald Stadium in Berlin, 1933

Today a new faith is awakening: the myth of blood, the faith to defend, by defending the blood, the divine essence of man. The faith embodied in the radiant knowledge that Nordic blood embodies that very mystery which has supplanted and vanquished the ancient sacraments.

Alfred Rosenberg

My measures will not be hindered by any legal considerations or bureaucracy whatsoever. It is not justice that I have to carry out but annihilation and extermination.

Hermann Goering in the Frankfurt Banqueting Hall, 4th March 1933

"Jew perish", Synagogue in Duesseldorf, 1933

Terror in Munich, 1933

For years the Hitlerites had scrawled their hate on to the walls of Jewish cemeteries and synagogues. They now put their threats into action.

This photograph of the lawyer Dr. Spiegel was published throughout the world Press: a man seeks police protection from SA terror. But the SA has been appointed "Auxiliary Police". Uniformed men lead their victim through the streets. The placard reads: "I shall *never* complain to the *police* again."

"Do not buy from Jews!" Berlin, 1st April 1933

Saturday's boycott is to be regarded merely as a dress-rehearsal for a series of measures that will be carried out unless world opinion, which at the moment is against us, definitely changes.

Voelkischer Beobachter, 3rd April 1933

The poster reads (*left*):

Jews are given until 10.0 a.m. on Saturday to reflect. Then the fight begins! The Jews of the world want to destroy Germany! German people! Defend yourselves! Do not buy from Jews!

*That was only a prelude,
where they burn books,
in the end it is men
that they burn.*

Heinrich Heine

The Burning of Books

Berlin, 11th May.—
Yesterday towards midnight the Berlin student body carried out their intention of publicly burning those books that they had taken out of the lending libraries in their *Aktion* "against the un-German spirit". The black-list compiled by them was very comprehensive. Not only Karl Marx, Bebel and Lassalle, Remarque, Renn and Tucholsky, Theodor Heuss, Rathenau and Gumbel, but also Schnitzler, Werfel and the Zweig brothers, among many others, were to be found on it.

Frankfurter Zeitung

19

Die Juden sind unser Unglüd

Frauen und Mädchen, die Juden sind Euer

Sports Palace in Berlin, 15th August 1935

Berlin, 16th August. Yesterday the leader of Franconia, *Gauleiter* Julius Streicher, spoke to an audience of about 16,000 in the Berlin Sports Palace. A further 5000 Berliners gathered in the Tennis Hall, the second largest hall in the capital, where the speech of Cde. Streicher was relayed over loudspeakers. Days before, tickets for both meetings were completely sold out . . . "What business is it of anybody else," asked Streicher, "if we are cleaning our house? . . . Nobody should trouble himself if we in Germany lead the defilers of our race through the streets to deter others . . . The Jewish question has not, as many people assume, been solved with the assumption of power by the National Socialists. *On the contrary, the hardest work is only just beginning.*"

Westdeutscher Beobachter

A Christian Fiancée of a Jew, Hamburg, 1935 *(right)*

(Doggerel on placard reads: I am the biggest swine in the place and only consort with Jews.)

The Nuremberg Race Laws and subsequent 20 decrees plunged thousands of families into misfortune and brought innumerable innocent people before the courts. A Jewish family employing a Christian domestic servant could be convicted of "racial ignominy", the same way an "Aryan" was liable to prosecution if, after these laws had been passed, he married a Jewish woman outside of Germany. The number of horrific convictions handed down by the German judicial system on the basis of the Nuremberg Laws has not been determined to this day. After a sentence of many years had been served in prison or penitentiary, transfer to a concentration camp was automatic, as was also the case for those convicted on political grounds. The pogrom of November 1938 signalled the beginning of persecution on a scale even more severe.

Berlin, 9th November 1938
Oranienburg Street Synagogue

Goering: How many synagogues were actually burnt down?

Heydrich: A total of 191 synagogues have been destroyed by fire, 76 demolished, 7500 shops destroyed in the *Reich* . . .

Goebbels: Then the Jews must pay for the damage . . .

Heydrich: Damage to property, equipment and stock is estimated at several hundred million (Marks) . . .

Goering: I wish you had killed 200 Jews instead of destroying so many valuables.

Heydrich: There are 35 dead.

Goering: I suggest we use the following wording, that the Jews, as a punishment for their abominable crimes, etc. etc. are made to contribute a hundred thousand Marks. That will do the trick.

Minutes of meeting in Goering's Ministry, 12th November 1938

Jewish Shop in Berlin after the Pogrom

Ninety-one people were killed on the night of the pogrom. More than 26,000 were carried off the next day to concentration camps. Now the laws followed in quick succession. Jews were not allowed to enter municipal parks or public squares. They were barred from visiting theatres, cinemas, concert halls and museums. Their children were expelled from the schools.

They lost their right to tenants' protection, they were not allowed to keep domestic animals, they had to report their assets, surrender their radios and all their jewellery. They were not allowed out after 8 o'clock at night. They were given specially marked identity cards.

"Aryans Only", Germany, 1938

Memel, 23rd March 1939

As happened in Austria and Czechoslovakia, the terror against the Jews began as soon as the Germans marched into Memel. Thousands fled to Lithuania.

These frightened children, holding their parents' hands as they fled to the station, had to run the gauntlet of grinning stormtroopers. The photograph appeared a few days later in the British Press.

Travel Agency, Meineke Street, Berlin, 1939

After the "Night of the Broken Glass", emigration, which had been increasing steadily since the Nuremberg Laws were passed, grew to a mass flight.

Over a quarter of a million people fled abroad to escape persecution. Many tried to reach Palestine in old charter steamers. But many ships found no port or were wrecked after going astray for weeks on end, in sight of the coast that was to save them.

Outside Shanghai

Before he could launch his predatory war against foreign peoples, Hitler had first to conquer the German people. He conquered them with banners and revolvers, the music of military bands and with concentration camps, with new places of work where people prepared for war, and with the property of Jewish neighbours.

After the democratic parties and unions had been prohibited and the bitterest opponents, the leaders of the organized workers' movement, had been killed, forced into exile, or put into concentration camps, the Nazis had clear sailing.

The best of the nation – the true patriots – stood up against injustice. They were many, but they were too few. The voice of conscience was drowned in the "*Sieg Heil*" roar of a crowd made fanatic – or was forcibly silenced. Germans were the first who passed through the concentration camps or underwent penal servitude in the prisons of the Third Reich.

Roll-call in Sachsenhausen Concentration Camp

Poland—Experimental Field of Operations

The denigration of the Jews as "subhumans" was in keeping with the concept of the Nordic "master-race" that possessed the natural right to conquer the world and enslave other nations. Once the dictator was established in his own country, expansion beyond the frontiers followed in accordance with a well-prepared plan.

Austria, Czechoslovakia and the District of Memel were just a curtain-raiser. The Second World War extended Hitler's dominion to the whole of Europe. One country after another was crushed by the German war machine. Everywhere the German occupation forces arrested the democratic politicians, oppressed the population, carried off millions to Germany for forced labour, and ruthlessly exploited the land to support the war economy.

The treatment of the Slav countries was particularly brutal. The Nazis regarded their peoples, next to the Jews, as an "inferior race", to be decimated and reduced to the status of slaves if the plan to exterminate them seemed impracticable.

Hundreds of thousands of people of all nations, millions of Polish, Serbian and Soviet citizens were killed by the Nazis in the course of this war. One section of the population, however, was almost completely exterminated—the Jews.

On 1st September 1939, Hitler's army invaded Poland. Over two million Jewish people fell into German hands. Heydrich's men, who had organised the "Night of the Broken Glass" in Germany, followed on the heels of the fighting forces to instigate pogroms everywhere.

The conquerors amused themselves by cutting off the beards of pious elderly Jews, making them do "gymnastics", robbing them and beating them up. They searched Jewish shops and homes "for weapons", smashed furniture and pocketed whatever took their fancy. Only in the Soviet-occupied part of Poland, the other side of the demarcation line, were the Jews protected for the time being.

After the terror and pillage of the first few weeks, the German civil administration began its legal war against the Jewish population with proclamations, decrees and announcements.

The wearing of the yellow-star insignia as a mark of identification by all Jews over the age of ten, the identification of shops, the reporting of assets, the introduction of forced labour, the banning from certain parts of the town, from parks and public squares, the exclusion from public transport—these were only the first of a whole series of measures, all directed towards the same end: to withdraw from the Jews the economic basis of their livelihood, to rob them and deprive them of all rights.

The persecuted people hoped at first that the Jewish Councils, set up on German orders, would afford them some protection from arbitrary action and represent their interests. In the course of time, however, these Councils degenerated into mere executive organs of the Occupation, and played an ambiguous and sometimes fateful role.

In the large towns, the Jews were forced to live in special walled-off residential districts. Thus the ghetto came into being—prison for hundreds of thousands, from which there was soon to be no return.

In October 1940 *Generalgouverneur* Frank ordered the establishment of ghettos throughout the country. The Jews in villages and small localities in the countryside were "resettled". Driven out of house and home, often with only the small baggage of the refugee, they walked long distances under guard to the ghetto of the nearest town. The elderly and sick followed behind on carts.

But soon the small ghettos were broken up again and the inhabitants concentrated in the large towns. The migration began again. Once more endless columns crowded the highways of Poland.

By the time they reached their destination, where overcrowded quarters awaited them, many had already lost the last of their few possessions, as well as their health. Step by step they sank to the lowest level of misery. Their social decline to beggary and dependence on public relief was inexorable. They would be the first to fall prey to starvation and disease, even before the mass deportations to the gas chambers began.

Nevertheless, again and again they bravely attempted to accept and adapt to the new conditions, in the vain hope that nothing worse could happen to them and that they would be spared greater catastrophe. But their situation was hopeless, and only death was certain.

Heydrich writes an Urgent Letter
To the Chiefs of all Einsatzgruppen of the Security Police   Berlin, 21.9.1939

Re: Jewish question in the occupied territory.

With reference to today's meeting in Berlin, I wish to stress once again that the *over-all measures projected* (the ultimate objective) are to be kept *strictly secret*.

Distinction must be made between
1. the ultimate objective (which is a long-term measure) and
2. the stages in the carrying out of the ultimate objective (which will be accomplished without delay).

The projected measures require the most thorough preparation, both technical and economic.

I

The first step towards the ultimate objective must be the concentration of the Jews from the countryside into the larger towns.

It is to be carried out at all speed.

It is absolutely necessary that Jewish communities of *less than* 500 people are broken up and concentrated in the nearest towns.

II

Jewish Councils of Elders
1. A Jewish Council of Elders is to be set up in every Jewish Community.
    It is to be made *fully responsible* in the full sense of the word for the exact and prompt carrying out of all past or current orders.
2. In the case of sabotage of such orders, the severest measures are to be announced to the council.
3. The Jewish Councils must undertake a provisional count of the Jews and communicate the result without delay.
4. The Councils of Elders are to be notified of the dates and time-limits, the facilities and finally the routes of the departure. They are then to be made personally responsible for the departure of the Jews from the countryside.
    The reason to be given for the concentration of the Jews in the towns is that Jews have taken a most prominent part in *franc-tireur* raids and looting activity.

Text of notice *(right)*:

The District Chief of Crackow

Identification of the Jews in the District of Crackow.

I hereby order that as from 1.12.1939 all Jews over the age of 12 years in the District of Crackow are to wear, outside their homes, a clearly visible mark of identification. This order also applies to Jews temporarily present in the District of Crackow for the duration of their stay.

For the purpose of this order, a Jew is considered to be:
1. whoever belongs or has belonged to the Mosaic religious community,
2. one whose father or mother belongs or has belonged to the Mosaic religious community.

The identification is to take the form of an armband, to be worn on the upper arm of clothing and outer clothing, bearing on its outer side a blue Star of David against a white background. The white background must be at least 10 cm. wide. The star must be of such a size that there is at least 8 cm. between the opposite points of the star. The lines forming the star must be at least 1 cm. wide.

Jews who do not fulfil this obligation are liable to severe punishment.

The Councils of Elders are responsible for the carrying out of this order, in particular for the supplying of the Jews with the identification insignia.

Crackow, 18.11.1939   signed—Waechter (Governor)

Der Distriktschef von Krakau

ANORDNUNG
Kennzeichnung der Juden im Distrikt Krakau

Ich ordne an, dass alle Juden im Alter von über 12 Jahren im Distrikt Krakau mit Wirkung vom 1. 12. 1939 ausserhalb ihrer eigenen Wohnung ein sichtbares Kennzeichen zu tragen haben. Dieser Anordnung unterliegen auch nur vorübergehend im Distriktsbereich anwesende Juden für die Dauer ihres Aufenthaltes.

Als Jude im Sinne dieser Anordnung gilt:

1. wer der mosaischen Glaubensgemeinschaft angehört oder angehört hat,

2. jeder, dessen Vater oder Mutter der mosaischen Glaubensgemeinschaft angehört oder angehört hat.

Als Kennzeichen ist am rechten Oberarm der Kleidung und der Überkleidung eine Armbinde zu tragen, die auf weissem Grunde an der Aussenseite einen blauen Zionstern zeigt. Der weisse Grund muss eine Breite von mindestens 10 cm. haben, der Zionstern muss so gross sein, dass dessen gegenüberliegende Spitzen mindestens 8 cm. entfernt sind. Der Balken muss 1 cm. breit sein.

Juden, die dieser Verpflichtung nicht nachkommen, haben strenge Bestrafung zu gewärtigen.

Für die Ausführung dieser Anordnung, insbesondere die Versorgung der Juden mit Kennzeichen, sind die Ältestenräte verantwortlich.

Krakau, den 18. 11. 1939.

gez. *Wächter*
Gouverneur

Szef dystryktu krakowskiego

ROZPORZĄDZENIE
Znamionowanie żydów w okręgu Krakowa

Zarządzam z ważnością od dnia 1. XII. 1939, iż wszyscy żydzi w wieku ponad 12 lat winni nosić widoczne znamiona. Rozporządzeniu temu podlegają także na czas ich pobytu przejściowo w obrębie okręgu przebywający żydzi.

Żydem w myśl tego rozporządzenia jest:

1) ten, który jest lub był wyznania mojżeszowego,

2) każdy, którego ojciec, lub matka są lub byli wyznania mojżeszowego.

Znamieniem jest biała przepaska noszona na prawym rękawie ubrania lub odzienia wierzchniego z niebieską gwiazdą sionistyczna. Przepaska winna mieć szerokość conajmniej 10 cm, a gwiazda średnice 8 cm. Wstążka, z której sporządzono gwiazdę, winna mieć szerokość conajmniej 1 cm.

Niestosujący się do tego zarządzenia zostaną surowo ukarani.

Za wykonanie niniejszego zarządzenia, zwłaszcza za dostarczenie opasek czynię odpowiedzialna Radę starszych.

Kraków, dnia 18. XI. 1939.

(—) *Wächter*
Gubernator

31

A Child keeps a Diary

21st March 1940. Early in the morning I was walking through the village where we live. From a long way off I saw a notice on the wall of the shop; I went up quickly to read it. The new notice said that Jews were not allowed to travel in vehicles any more (it has been forbidden to go on trains for a long time).

4th April 1940. I got up earlier today because I wanted to go to Kielce. I left the house after· breakfast. I felt unhappy going through the lanes alone like that. After walking for four hours, I arrived in Kielce. When I got to my uncle's house, I saw that they were all sitting there depressed, and heard that the Jews had been evacuated from different streets, and I was overcome with sadness too.

5th April 1940. I could not sleep all night. Strange thoughts were going through my head. After breakfast I went home.

9th June 1940. Today there were German military exercises. All the soldiers were scattered over the fields. They set up machine guns and shot at each other.

18th June 1940. The police searched our house today for some military things or other. The policeman asked me where the things were and I answered all the time that there weren't any and that was that. Anyway they did not find anything and went away again.

5th August 1940. Yesterday the watchman from the parish council called in at the mayor's— all Jews had to go with their families and register at the council building. We were already there at 7 o'clock in the morning. We were there for several hours. Then the older ones elected a Council of Elders. Then we went home.

12th August 1940. Ever since the war I have been studying at home on my own. When I think of how I used to go to school, I could cry. But now I must sit here. I'm not allowed to go out anywhere. And when I think what wars are going on in the world, and how many people are killed every day by bullets, gas, bombs, epidemics and other enemies of man, I lose interest in everything.

1st September 1940. Today is the first anniversary of the outbreak of war. I am thinking about all that has happened to us in this short time, how much misfortune we have had already . . .

10th July 1941. A very hard time has begun. It is difficult to get through a single hour. We always used to have a little food put by, at least enough for a month. But now it is difficult to buy enough food for one day. A day does not go by but someone comes begging. Everybody who comes wants something to eat, nothing else, which is now the most difficult thing.

26th December 1941. An order has been issued that the Jews must hand over all furs, even small pieces. And five Jews will have to answer for anyone who will not hand them over. The order is so harsh that anyone who is seen or found with furs will be sentenced to death. The police have set a deadline of 4 o'clock this afternoon.

8th January 1942. I learned this afternoon that there were two more victims among the Jews in Bodzentyn. One was already dead, the other wounded. They have arrested the one who was wounded and taken him to the guard-room in Bieliny. They will beat him to death there.

11th January 1942. Since early morning there have been snowstorms and heavy frost. Today the temperature was 20 deg. Celsius. As I was watching the wind sweeping over the fields, I noticed that the village watchman was pasting up a notice. I went at once to see what was new. There was nothing new on the notice. The watchman only said that he had brought notices to the mayor that all Jews had to be evacuated from all villages. When I told them at home, we were all very depressed. Now, in such a hard winter, they are going to evacuate us. Where? Where to? Now our turn has come to bear great suffering. The Lord knows, how long for.

Entries made by David Rubinowicz,
who was gassed in Treblinka at the age of 14

Hitler outside Warsaw

And so we National Socialists are deliberately drawing a line under the foreign policy of our pre-war period. We are starting where they left off 600 years ago. We are putting an end to the eternal movement of Germanic people to Southern and Western Europe, and turning our eyes towards the East.

Adolf Hitler, Mein Kampf

33

SS "Barbers" *(right)*

Forced Labour in Conquered Warsaw

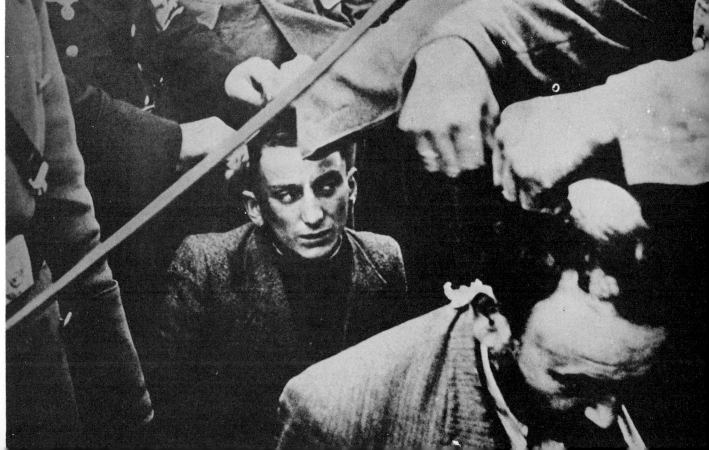

They taunted and tormented defenceless people and posed for the photograph album. "Wireless operator Griese instructs Lublin Jews with raised stick", wrote a soldier under this photograph. There was worse to follow: arrests, interrogations and the shooting of hostages (*pages 38—39*).

Execution of Hostages in Zdunska Wola, Poland

Pogrom in Kovno, Lithuania *(left)*

The Security Police, which directed pogroms in all the occupied towns in the East, at first kept themselves in the background. In the blood bath in Kovno, on 28th June 1941, they had hundreds of Jews beaten to death with iron bars by freed convicts.

"Resettlement" was the name given to the next phase. Jews were thrown out of their homes, turned out into the street and led off into the ghettos.

Turned out

As from now, a closed-off Jewish residential district is to be established in the Crackow area, in which all Jews living in the town must take up residence. All Jews without exception are forbidden to live outside the Jewish residential district.

Dr. Waechter, Chief of the District of Crackow

42

In accordance with the Decree on the Limitation of Residence in the *Generalgouvernement* of 13th September 1940 (V. BL. G. G. I. S. 288), a Jewish residential district will be established in Warsaw, in which the Jews living in or moving into the city of Warsaw are to take up residence.

Dr. Fischer, Chief of the District of Warsaw

Led away

Resettlement in Mielec

On 11th March 1942, a transport comprising 2000 Jews leaves Mielec, destination Parczew and Miedzyrzec. One thousand Jews are to be unloaded at each destination. Arrival in Parczew, 12th March, 5.53 hours. They will stop there until 8.22 hours. Arrival in Miedzyrzec, 12th March, 12 noon. Next transport probably leaves Friday. Details of journey will be made known in due course.

Major Ragger, Crackow, to the Governor of the District of Lublin, 10th March 1942

44

On Sunday, 14th March 1942, a transport comprising 2000 Jews leaves Mielec, destination Hrubieszow and Susiec. It will be divided at Zamosc. Arrival of that part with destination Hrubieszow comprising 1500 Jews, Monday, 16th March 1942, 13.05 hours. Arrival of that part with destination Susiec comprising 500 Jews, Monday. 16th March 1942, 13.12 hours. *Aktion* Evacuation of Jews from Kielec is now completed.

Major Ragger, Crackow, to the Governor of the District of Lublin, 13th March 1942

"Resettlement" was a constantly recurring procedure. As the latest ghetto was established, the first ones were already being broken up and combined in the next, larger town of the district, until finally the last journey began. At the time when the ghettos in the big towns were still temporarily in existence, in the country whole Jewish communities were already being transported to the death camps.

Lodz

The Jews of the countless little towns were herded together, the flat countryside cleansed of isolated Jewish families living there. One icy winter evening towards the end of the first year of the war, an endless column of Jewish inhabitants of a small country town was driven to the well-known town of Brzeziny, about 30 kilometres to the east. The farm carts accompanying the column carried, together with the children, the aged and the sick, the pitiful luggages of the evacuees. Mutely these people walked through the bitterly cold night—a picture of suffering and patience. Mute, too, the Jews in Lodz itself, moved in for a whole week, from all directions, laden only with hand baggage, into the central ghetto, the domicile that had been assigned to the quarter of a million of them. Again it was on a bad winter night that Special Detachments combed the Jewish houses for those who had remained behind. Anyone who did not vacate his home immediately was shot down. There were many: the shots, that sounded continuously, as in a battle, testified to that. No-one was allowed to leave his home during the hours of the night, so one discovered only the next morning what a battle had raged.

The Rev. Schedler, Wuerzburg (formerly Lodz)

47

Swietokrzyska Street in Warsaw

The great wall was built with Jewish money. The Jewish Council had to pay a German firm of builders for the materials and building costs. The firm owned the concession for building the ghetto wall, which was built to a thickness of two bricks. Sharp pieces of glass were set into the mortar to prevent anybody climbing the wall.

Statement by Jonas Turkow

48

In the Ghettos

Ghettos were transit stations on the road to death. For many they were the last station.

At first people still went to their usual place of work in the "Aryan" part of the town, returning to the ghetto at night. One day the ghetto was closed off with barbed wire and armed sentries posted at the gates.

The cutting off of the ghetto from the outside world brought economic disaster. The small workshops within the enclosure could only provide work for a few. Hundreds of thousands were imprisoned in a huge cage, abandoned to certain death by starvation to which Hitler had condemned them. And still more and more masses of people were crammed into the already overcrowded ghettos.

Here too, confiscation of property, bullying, beatings, looting, wild shooting and public executions never ceased. There was one tribulation, however, so terrible that all others paled beside it—starvation. Starvation was the lament of the beggars, sitting in the street with their homeless families. Starvation was the cry of the mothers whose new-born babies wasted away and died. Men fought tooth and nail over a raw potato. Children risked their lives smuggling in a handful of turnips for which whole families were waiting.

In the end, the total month's ration in Warsaw consisted of 2 lb. of bread, 9 oz. of sugar, $3\frac{1}{2}$ oz. of jam and $1\frac{3}{4}$ oz. of fats. Often food was delivered that had been rejected by the army as unfit for human consumption. People tried with diligence and ingenuity to relieve the suffering. Hand-made goods were laboriously produced in primitive workshops to barter in the "Aryan" part of the town. Useful kitchen utensils were made from pieces of wood, old sheets were transformed into brightly printed table-cloths. Whole lorryloads of provisions were smuggled into the ghetto with the help of sentries, who extorted enormous bribes from the starving people. In spite of this, the death rate rose constantly. Spotted fever broke out in the slum districts. Carts came round collecting corpses more and more often. But soon the German authorities' order that corpses must not lie in the street for more than 15 minutes could no longer be observed. Those dying from exhaustion lay down in the gutter, and the living passed by without looking round. Poverty, hunger and despair gnawed deeper and deeper until there was nothing left.

A still worse fate awaited those who did not die in the ghetto. In July 1942 transportation to the extermination camps began. Extermination by starvation was followed with extermination by gas. The Jewish Councils were forced to compile transportation lists. From Warsaw alone 400,000 people in three months were transported to Belsec and Treblinka. Mass refugee shelters, hospitals and orphanages were the first to be evacuated. Then it was the turn of everyone not engaged in war work. At first, many of the homeless came forward voluntarily, just to get the half-loaf and tin of jam that everyone was promised for the journey. So great was their need that they did not even fear the concentration camps, where at least they could hope for a bed at night and a bowl of food.

Later, when the first rumours about the gas chambers penetrated the ghetto, brute force had to be used to drive the terrified people into the wagons. For days on end the town was like a jungle where a wild manhunt was going on. The streets re-echoed with the curses of the police and the screams of their victims. Beaten and bloody, they were dragged, kicking and struggling, to the "Umschlagplatz". Crammed by the hundred into cattle wagons, many died on the journey. When the pressure on Treblinka became too great, the sealed trains were left on the track for days until all the occupants were suffocated.

In the summer of 1943 the ghettos, with the exception of "Litzmannstadt" (Lodz), were finally broken up. Only a few companies of Jewish prisoners in forced labour camps remained. They too, sooner or later, went to the execution pits or the gas chambers.

"The Creation of a Ghetto"—Lodz

In my opinion, there are approximately 320,000 Jews living in Lodz today. Their immediate evacuation is not possible. Thorough enquiries at all the relevant administrative departments have shown that the concentration of all Jews in an enclosed ghetto is possible . . .

After completion of these preparatory measures and with sufficient guard forces placed in readiness, the establishment of the ghetto shall take place without warning at a date to be determined by me, that is, at an appointed hour, the stipulated boundaries of the ghetto will be occupied by the guard personnel assigned to that purpose, and the streets closed by *cheval-de-frises* and other devices for the closing of thoroughfares. Simultaneously, the walling up or shutting off by other means of the house-fronts will commence, using a Jewish labour force to be drawn from the ghetto. In the ghetto itself a self-governing administration will be set up . . .

Circular letter from Uebelhoer, President of the Administrative District of Kalisch

"An Outside View of the Jewish Residential District"—Warsaw

The Jewish residential district covers about 403 hectares (approx. $1\frac{3}{5}$ sq. miles). According to the statements of the Jewish Council, which claims to have carried out a census, about 410,000 Jews live in this district. According to our observations and estimates, made from different sides, there are about 470,000–590,000 Jews.

On the basis of the statistics given by the Jewish Council, and allowing for areas of ground and cemeteries, 1108 persons live on one hectare of built-on area, i.e. 110,800 persons per sq. km. The density of population in the City of Warsaw amounts to 14,400 persons per sq. km. of total area and 38,000 per sq. km. of built-on and habitable area.

It should be noted that the number is increased by 72,000 Jews, due to the fact that a resettlement measure from the western part of the district has again become necessary. Room must be found for 62,000 evacuated Poles.

In the Jewish residential district there are about 27,000 dwellings with an average of $2\frac{1}{2}$ rooms per dwelling. Occupancy can be calculated, therefore, at 15.1 persons per dwelling and 6 to 7 persons per room.

The Jewish residential district is separated from the rest of the city by fireproof and dividing walls and by the walling up of street-blocks, windows, doors and spaces between buildings. The walls are 3 metres high and are raised a further metre by a barbed-wire fixture.

In addition, motorised and mounted police patrols keep the area under surveillance.

Report by Waldemar Schoen, Resettlement Officer to the District Governor of Warsaw

The described increase in food supplies could not prevent the rise in the number of deaths, which is due to the over-all impoverishment of the Jews that has existed since the beginning of the war. The following figures give a striking picture of the deaths:

January 41	898	May 41	3821
February 41	1023	June 41	4290
March 41	1608	July 41	5550
April 41	2061	August 41	5560

Another reason for this increase in the mortality rate is the outbreak of spotted fever in the Jewish residential district. Despite strenuous efforts to combat the spotted fever, the curve has risen steadily. Since about July of this year the weekly notifications of cases of spotted fever have remained fairly constant. They vary between 320 and 450 new cases. The figure for last month (August) of 1788 persons is not significantly higher than that for the previous month, with 1736.

Report by Heinz Auerswald, Commissar for the Jewish Residential District in Warsaw

The City of Death

The streets are so over-populated, it is difficult to push one's way through. Everyone is ragged, in tatters. Often they no longer even possess a shirt. Everywhere there is noise and uproar. The thin piteous voices of children crying their wares—"Pretzels, cigarettes, sweets!"—are heard above the din.

No-one will ever be able to forget those children's voices.

There are heaps and piles of filth and refuse on the pavements. Often a child will snatch a packet from a passer-by and run away, ravenous over the food inside. Even when he is caught and beaten, the young creature will not give up his meal.

I see an enormous number of men, women and children being hounded by the police. When I approach and ask what is going on, I learn that they are refugees, dragging with them their last possessions—a bundle, a cushion or just a straw mattress. They were thrown out of their homes at five minutes' notice and not allowed to take anything with them. They come from the small towns in the surrounding district. Old people and cripples, the sick and infirm were liquidated on the spot. Anybody who does not keep pace and falls behind is despatched on the march. Should a son stay behind with his murdered father, he is also killed in the same way. The tragic expressions on the faces of these refugees vary between fear of death and resignation . . .

Often there is something lying on the pavement, covered with newspaper. Emaciated limbs or morbidly swollen legs usually stick out from underneath. These are the corpses of the spotted typhus victims. The other people living in the house simply carry them outside because they cannot afford the burial expenses. Or it may be one of the homeless paupers who has collapsed in the street.

Every opening in the wall is guarded. The guard consists of a few Germans, who look at the crowd with contempt, Polish police and the Jewish police. These last are slapped in the face if they do not carry out their orders properly.

There are always countless children inside the ghetto. People on the "Aryan" side gape curiously at the piteous spectacle presented by these tattered gangs. In fact, these gangs of children are the ghetto breadwinners. If the German looks away for one second, they run nimbly over to the "Aryan" side. The bread, potatoes and other things that they buy there are hidden under their rags, and then they have to slip back the way they came . . .

Not all the German sentries are murderers and executioners but, unfortunately, many of them do not hestitate to take up their guns and fire at the children. Every day—it is almost unbeliev-able—children are taken to hospital with gunshot wounds.

All Jews must wear the armband with its Star of David. The children are the only exceptions, and this makes it easier for them to smuggle food in. Often, in less than no time, they will throw small packets into the ghetto from the tramway that runs along the "Aryan" side of the street just as the tram is passing the gate of the ghetto, and then jump in themselves.

The children also climb over the wall, but this must be done very quickly, lest one of the sentries chooses that moment to look round. If he sees this happening, he shoots immediately . . .

The thousands of ragged beggars are reminiscent of a famine in India. Horrifying sights are to be seen every day. Here a half-starved mother is trying to suckle her baby at a breast that has no milk. Beside her may lie another, older child, dead. One sees people dying, lying with arms and legs outstretched, in the middle of the road. Their legs are bloated, often frost-bitten, and their faces distorted with pain. I hear that every day the beggar children's frost-bitten fingers and toes, hands and feet are amputated . . .

I once asked a little girl: "What would you like to be?" "A dog," she answered, "because the sentries like dogs."

The Jews who work in "Aryan" sectors are given passes in order to get to their place of work. They have to pass the guard at the double, hat in hand. Sometimes the sentries stop a group and order them to undress and grovel in the dirt. They also like to make them do "knee-bends". Some-times they even have to dance. The sentries stand by and almost kill themselves laughing.

From the sketches of Prof. Ludwik Hirszfeld, Warsaw

Re: Hunger

Re: Food situation in the ghetto
It must be pointed out that the report that the population of the ghetto is better fed than is justifiable is misleading and erroneous. In 1940 the rations for about 200,000 Jews stood at the level of the quota for prisoners. For more than a year now, the rations have been below the quota allotted to prisoners. Nobody can maintain that the inhabitants of the ghetto remain for long capable of utilisation as labour on the existing rations. In fact, the state of health of the Jews is deteriorating daily because the quotas that appear on paper simply cannot be fulfilled as market conditions do not allow this. Moreover, everything that comes into the ghetto in the way of provisions is, as a rule, of inferior quality. Damaged goods (vegetables, fats, cereal products, etc.) are constantly being unloaded on to the ghetto but are, nevertheless, fully included in the quota. The clearest demonstration of the food situation is the rapidly rising mortality rate.

Amtsleiter Biebow, Ghetto Administration, to the Litzmannstadt Gestapo, 4.3.1942.

Re: Jewish rations
As the undersigned has already explained to you personally, the rations provided for the Jews are no longer justifiable in their present form because otherwise a loss of efficiency detrimental to the armed forces will ensure. In the workshops and factories where, due to a shortage of skilled workers, 12-hour shift-working (day and night) has been introduced, the workers, especially those who have to work standing up, are now collapsing at their places of work.

During the last evacuation, in September 1942, all sick and infirm Jews were transferred else-where. In spite of this, mortality figures for the period from that time until 31.3.43 amount to 4658.

Amtsleiter Biebow, Ghetto Administration, to the Chief Burgomaster of Litzmannstadt, 19.4.1943

Special Order in Respect of Use of Firearms *while guarding the Litzmannstadt Ghetto*

Under No. 9 of the Special Instructions issued by the Chief of Police concerning contact with the ghetto (Instr. S 1a dated 10.5.40), in the case of any attempt by a Jewish inhabitant of the ghetto to leave the ghetto in any unauthorised manner whatsoever, immediate use of firearms is to be made. With the endorsement of the Chief of Police, I hereby amplify the order as follows:

1. The use of firearms in a crowded street incurs the strong possibility of wounding a party not involved. This is to be avoided.
2. Any person who merely approaches the ghetto fence from the outside in a suspicious manner is to be challenged with the word "Halt". Only if the person challenged does not stand still on being challenged, or tries to run away, is shooting to take place.
3. Any Jew who tries to crawl through or to climb over the ghetto fence, or attempts to leave the ghetto in any other unauthorised manner, is to be shot without challenge.
4. Any Jew who throws any kind of smuggled article or money over the fence, or receives objects thrown over the fence, if he is caught *in the act*, is to be shot without challenge.
5. Any Jew who loiters right by the fence after the curfew (21.00 hours) is to be shot without challenge.
6. Any person caught *in the act* of smuggling goods, money, etc. into the ghetto from the outside, or receiving same, is to be shot without challenge.
7. Any person caught *in the act* of crawling through or climbing over the fence from the outside is to be shot without challenge.

Special Order of the Police in Litzmannstadt Ghetto, 11th April 1941

Re: Robbery

The *Reichsfuehrer-SS* Himmler has ordered the collection of all fur-coats, furs and hides of any kind whatsoever that have been found amongst and confiscated from Jews; together with those of still existing Jews, which are about to be confiscated immediately, particularly in the ghettos in the *Generalgouvernement*. The number is to be regularly reported to me by teleprinter from 29.12.1941, not later than 18.00 hours. The *Reichsfuehrer* has commanded that his order be carried out without delay (underlined) . . . The Jewish Councils are to be warned that they themselves, with any Jews caught in possession of a fur or hide after the lapse of a stipulated period, will be shot.

The Chief of the Security Police in the Generalgouvernement, to the District Chiefs of the SS and Police, 24th December 1941

Re: *Aktion* in respect of Jews in Piaski
I attach two statements regarding goods secured from the ghetto in Piaski. While some of the effects withdrawn from the Hessian Jews are as new, the remaining textiles consist of fairly old and dirty fabric for the rag-chopping machine. The articles of clothing of the Hessian Jews are packed in cases. In addition, up till now, a sum of 8300 zloties (partly in *Reichsmarks*), 85 gold roubles, as well as five wedding rings has been secured.
   As the store-rooms are urgently required for other purposes, I would ask for early collection.

Security Police, Piaski Transfer Office, to the Chief of Security Police in Lublin, 11th April 1942

Re: Jewish labour camp—Pabianice
The superabundant supply of textiles, shoes, etc., from the Warthbruecken resettlement camp and the evacuated ghettos necessitates the addition of further store-rooms.
   For this purpose, the Polish churches in Alexanderhof and Erzhausen have been placed at my disposal by the Gestapo . . .

Ghetto Administration to the Chief of Police of Litzmannstadt, 8th June 1942

Re: Delivery of textile goods to the NSV (Nazi Welfare Organisation) by the Ghetto Administration
A large proportion of the articles of clothing is heavily patched and in some cases also saturated with dirt and blood stains . . . The crates were forwarded unopened from the Litzmannstadt district office to different district offices in the region, so it was not discovered until later, when the crates were opened, that in a delivery to the Poznan Office, for example, the Jewish star had not been removed from 51 out of 200 coats! As in the district warehouses mainly Polish warehousemen have to be employed, there is a danger that the returning emigrants, provided for by the WHW (Winter Welfare Organisation), may come to know the source of the clothing and the WHW will be brought into disrepute as a result . . .

Regional representative of the Poznan WHW, to the Litzmannstadt Ghetto Administration, 9th January 1943

Re: Disposal of second-hand articles by the Ghetto Administration
An inventory of all the goods and second-hand articles accruing as a result of evacuation measures, and still on hand (furs, clothing, jewellery and household articles, etc.), is to be drawn up and submitted to me. The term ''second-hand articles'' is to be applied in its widest sense. The inventory is to be regularly kept up to date with new additions.

Ventzki, Chief Burgomaster of Litzmannstadt, to the Ghetto Administration, 20th September 1943

"Evacuation"

On the night of 13/14th July 1942, all the inhabitants of the ghetto in Rovno, where there were still about 5000 Jews, were liquidated . . .

Shortly after 22.00 hours, the ghetto was surrounded by a large body of the SS and about three times as many Ukrainian militia. The arc-lamps erected in and around the ghetto were then switched on. Groups of four to six SS and militiamen then forced or tried to force their way into the houses. Where the doors and windows were locked, and the occupants did not open up at the knocking and shouting, the SS and militiamen broke the windows in and broke open the doors with wooden beams and crowbars, and forced their way in. The inhabitants were driven out into the street just as they were, whether they were dressed or had been in bed. As most of the Jews resisted and refused to leave their homes, the SS and militia used force. With lashes of the whip, kicks and rifle-butt blows, they finally succeeded in evacuating the houses. People were driven out with such haste that in some cases young children were left behind in bed. In the street, women were weeping and crying for their children, children for their parents. This did not prevent the SS from driving and beating them through the streets at the double until they reached the waiting goods train. Wagon after wagon was filled. There was a continuous screaming of women and children, cracking of whips and rifle-shots. As individual families or groups of people had barricaded themselves in houses that were particularly sound, and the doors could not be broken down by means of crow-bars and beams, they were blown up with hand-grenades. The railway line out of Rovno ran close by the ghetto, and some young people tried to escape from the ghetto area over the railway lines and across a small river. As this stretch of land lay outside the area lit by the arc-lamps, signal rockets were used to illuminate it. Throughout the night these people, beaten, hounded and wounded, trailed through the brightly lit streets. Women carried dead children in their arms. Children hauled and dragged their dead parents by the arms and legs through the streets to the train. Again and again, the shouts of "Open up! Open up!" echoed and re-echoed through the ghetto.

Friedrich Graebe, a German witness

From the street beyond the gate came the familiar sounds of the killers, loud wild shouting and the clatter of hobnailed boots. Searchlights swept the yard. I dashed into an open doorway and up a flight of steps. Below me a searchlight caught the doorway, then the stairs, and paused. I scrambled higher. Hobnailed boots were already on the steps.

I reached the attic and felt my way in the dark. The headboard of a broken bed leaned against the wall. I crawled behind it and stumbled into a human body. It was warm and trembling. Whoever it was, he was alive and as frightened as I.

The space was not big enough for two of us, but it was too late to turn back and look elsewhere. I could not have if I had wanted to, for my companion clutched me in convulsive fear. It was a woman. She was breathing heavily and trying hard to stifle her gasps. We pressed against the wall. She twisted close to me and her chin dug into my shoulder. Her heart was pounding heavily. She did not say a word; I heard only her muffled breathing.

Several times they came into the attic and flashed their lights about. We crouched, trembling, expecting that at any moment the light would pick us out. Each time we heard the hobnails on the steps she tightened her grip on me. Each time her heart beat more wildly. Both of us shivered spasmodically.

Through my mind raced the fear that she would have a heart attack at any moment, and that she would die here with her arms clutched tightly around me.

Again the damned boots came. *"Hier ist niemand. Wir waren schon hier."* The clatter faded into the distance. A deathly stillness descended around us. For a moment, at least, we were safe.

Bernard Goldstein, a Jewish survivor

Bekanntmachung Nr. 428.

Betr.: Verkleinerung des Gettos.

Zusätzlich zu den bisher gesperrten Wohngebieten der Juden lt. Bekanntmachung Nr. 427 v. 17. August 1944 sind mit sofortiger Wirkung

bis spätestens 24. August 1944, 7 Uhr früh

nachstehend bezeichnete Gebiete restlos zu r ä u m e n.

Die in diesen Gebieten wohnenden Personen haben ihre Wohnungen bis zum genannten Termin zu verlassen und dürfen die geräumten Gebiete

NICHT MEHR BETRETEN.

Wer dieser Aufforderung nicht Folge leistet und am Donnerstag, .24. August 1944, nach 7 Uhr früh in diesen Gebieten sowie in den bereits geräumten noch angetroffen wird, wird

mit dem Tode bestraft.

Es handelt sich

um das Gebiet begrenzt; im Westen längs der Siegfriedstrasse von Nr. 7 — Nr. 85 also von der Ecke Sulzfelderstrasse—Siegfriedstrasse bis Ecke Siegfriedstrasse—Robertstrasse.

begrenzt: im Norden längs der Robertstrasse ungerade Nummern also von der Ecke Siegfriedstrasse—Robertstrasse bis zur Ecke Robertstrasse—Maxstrasse. (Polenjugendverwahrlager).

begrenzt: im Osten längs der Maxstrasse also von der Ecke Robertstrasse — Maxstrasse bis zur Ecke Maxstrasse—Ewaldstrasse (längs des Westzaunes des Polenjugendverwahrlagers). Von dieser Ecke weiter nach Osten längs der Ewaldstrasse bis zum Gettozaun.

begrenzt: im Osten längs der Gewerbestrasse also längs des Gettozaunes.

begrenzt: im Süden durch die Winfriedstrasse also längs des Gettozaunes.

begrenzt: im Osten durch die Konradstrasse also längs des Gettozaunes bis zur Sulzfelderstr.

und im Süden längs der Sulzfelderstrasse also von der Ecke Siegfriedstrasse—Sulzfelderstrasse bis zur Ecke Sulzfelderstrasse — Konradstrasse (also Sulzfelderstrasse von Nr. 70—100 — Schluss der Sulzfelderstrasse).

Zur besonderen Beachtung:

Die in diesen Gebieten in geschlossenen Betrieben kasernierten Arbeiter können an ihrem Arbeitsplatz verbleiben und dürfen in Ausübung ihrer Dienstpflichten die Gebiete betreten.

Dasselbe gilt für das Krankenhaus.

GEHEIME STAATSPOLIZEI.

Litzmannstadt,
d. 22. 8. 1944.

A Letter

On the tenth day of the *"Aktion"* in Warsaw Mother went to Treblinka. It was like this:

Early one morning—it was Friday—Mother came to Nalevky Street, where I am living with Cywia and Izak. She brought us food and was longing for us. When she set off home on her own, I was anxious about her because the man-hunt always began at 7'clock. I went with her as far as the gate, did some shopping in the town and came home again. I had not yet finished lunch, when a comrade came running in from the Arnim "Kibbutz" and cried: "Mordecai, they've got your mother."

I ran at once to Leszno Street but the bus had already gone. So I ran on to the *"Umschlagplatz"* and promised the police money if they looked for Mother. But they did not find her. Probably she had been too afraid to report. Only when she was already in the bus did she shout, "Go and tell them at 34 Dzielna Street!"

Well, they brought the news, but what use was that? To be honest, I must admit that I did not do all I could to get her out. They would have got her anyway one day. Tomorrow, next week—next month. Of course she had all the work permits and papers possible. But it made no difference. She would have to be nabbed one day. Every one of us must—*must*—go sooner or later. One way or another. It can't be helped. Every day thousands of mothers, fathers and children are dragged off. Why should our mother be an exception . . .

Last news from M. Tennenbaum to his sister in Palestine, July 1943

An Appeal

In the Warsaw Ghetto, behind the wall which cuts it off from the world, several hundred thousand condemned are awaiting death. For them there is no hope of rescue, no help is coming to them from anywhere. The executioners speed through the streets, shooting anyone who dares to leave his house. They also shoot anyone who appears at the window. Unburied bodies lie about the roads. The prescribed daily number of victims is eight to ten thousand. The Jewish police are obliged to hand them over to the German executioners. If they fail to do so they themselves perish. Children who are not strong enough to walk are loaded on to carts. The loading is done so brutally that few reach the siding alive . . . Railway trucks wait at the siding. The executioners thrust up to 150 condemned persons into each. A thick layer of lime and chlorine, over which water has been poured, is spread over the floors. The truck doors are sealed. Sometimes the train sets off immediately it is loaded, sometimes it stands in a siding for a couple of days. That is of no matter to anyone now. Of the people packed in so tightly that the dead cannot fall and continue to stand shoulder to shoulder with the living, of the people slowly dying in the fumes of lime and chlorine, deprived of air, a drop of water, food, none will be left alive . . .

In the face of this torture only a speedy death would be emancipation. The executioners have foreseen this. All chemists shops in the Ghetto have been closed so that they shall not supply poison.

What is happening in the Warsaw Ghetto has been happening for six months past in a hundred smaller and larger Polish towns. The total number of Jews killed already exceeds a million, and the figure is rising every day. Everybody is perishing. Rich and poor, old people and women, men, youngsters, infants . . . all guilty of having been born in the Jewish nation are condemned by Hitler to extermination.

We do not wish to be like Pilate. We cannot actively oppose the German murderers; we can do nothing, we can save nobody. But from the bottom of our hearts, filled with compassion, loathing and horror, we protest. That protest is demanded of us by God, by God who forbade killing. It is demanded by the Christian conscience. Every creature calling himself a man has the right to the love of his neighbour. The blood of the helpless calls to heaven for vengeance. Anyone who does not support this protest is no Catholic . . .

Illegal leaflet of the "Front for the Restoration of Poland"

Ghetto Entrance, Lodz

The ghetto is obviously only a temporary measure. At what juncture and by what means the ghetto, and thereby the town of Lodz, will be cleansed of Jews, I reserve to myself. Our final objective must be, in any case, to burn out this plague boil without trace.

signed: Uebelhoer

57

Pass Inspection

Re: Use of fire-arms

On 1st December 1941, I was on duty between 14.00 and 16.00 hours at Sentry Post No. 4 in Holstein Street. At 15.00 hours, I saw a Jewess climb on to the fence of the ghetto, stick her head through the fence and attempt to steal turnips from a passing cart. I made use of my fire-arm. The Jewess received two fatal shots. Type of fire-arm: Carbine 98. Ammunition used: two cartridges.

Report of Wachtmeister Naumann, Litzmannstadt, 1st December 1941

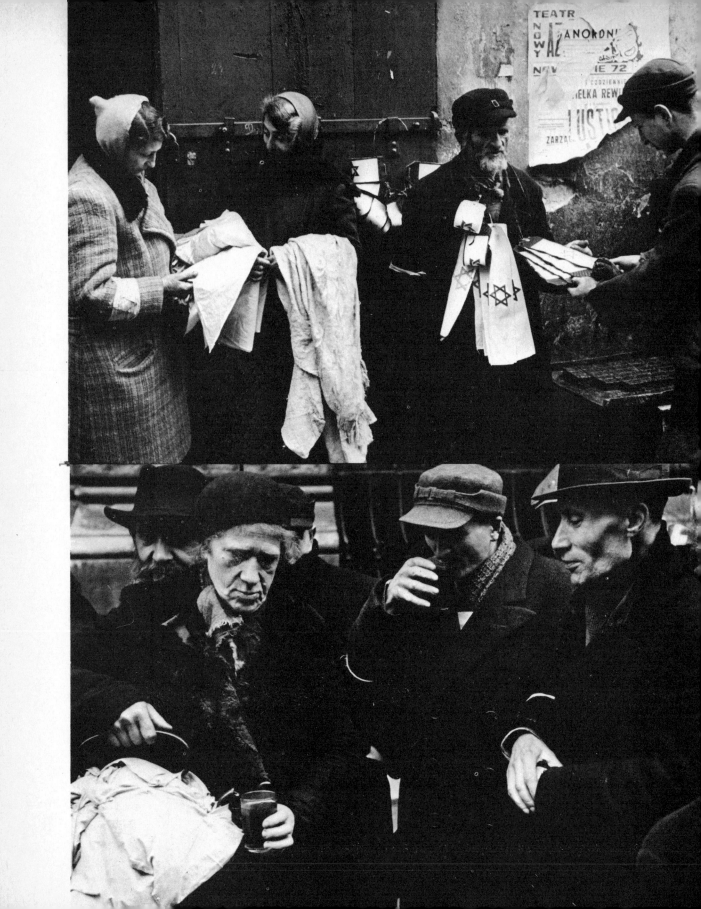

Once when I was walking along by the wall, I came across a "smuggling operation" being carried out by children. The actual "operation" seemed to be over. There was only one thing left to do. The little Jewish boy on the other side of the wall had to slip back into the ghetto through his hole, bringing with him the last piece of booty. Half of the little boy was already visible, when he began to cry out. At the same time loud abuse in German could be heard from the "Aryan" side. I hurried to help the child, meaning to pull him quickly through the hole. Unhappily, the boy's hips stuck fast in the gap in the wall. Using both hands, I tried with all my might to pull him through. He continued to scream dreadfully. I could hear the police on the other side beating him savagely. When I finally succeeded in pulling the boy through the hole, he was already dying. His backbone was crushed.

Statement by W. Szpilman

Begging for a Crust of Bread

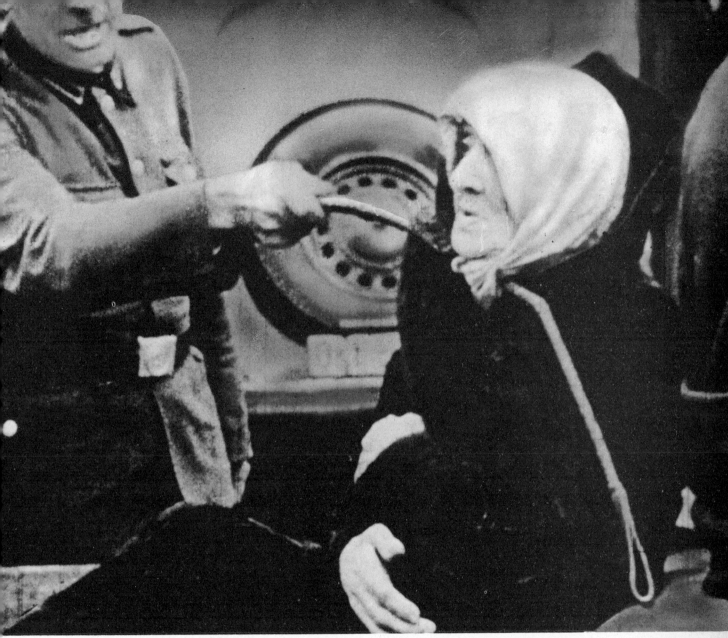

Tormenting and beating Jews in the Ghettos of Lemberg, Minsk *(left)* **and Warsaw**

The slandering foreign journalists, who so frequently write such drivel about alleged barbaric persecution of Jews in the German East, are strongly recommended to satisfy themselves on the spot as to the liberal manner in which the German Administration allows the Jews to pursue their own way of life.

Dr. Max Freiherr du Prel

Jews received one-twelfth of the food ration to which Germans were entitled and had to pay twenty times the price. The Jewish Social Self-Help Organisation tried to relieve the distress as best it could and distributed hot soup once a day to the poorest of the poor. For 100,000 people this was their only meal. But the army of the starving continued to grow, and the soup became thinner and thinner, until in the end it consisted merely of hay and hot water. A child welfare agency found homes for 5,000 homeless orphans and organized the feeding of a further 30,000, but, of approximately 100,000 children in the Warsaw ghetto, the vast majority did not receive any aid.

Soup Kitchen

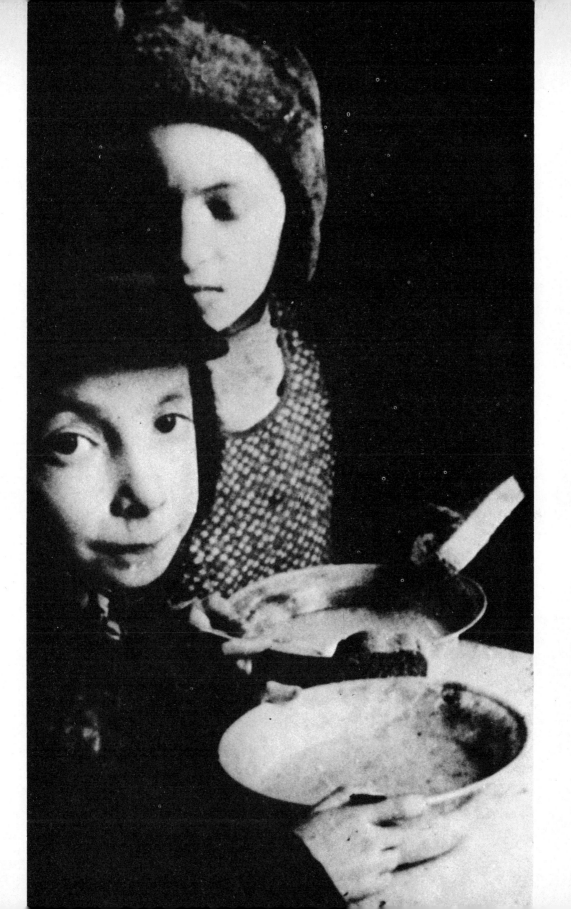

Death in the Street

Forced Labour *(left)*

Under the harsh living conditions, to do twelve hours' forced labour was a privilege. The gangs of workers, who were transported to the "Aryan" part of the town every morning, at least received something to eat. But fewer and fewer had the strength to withstand heavy physical exertion. Sooner or later, they too collapsed from exhaustion, like the unemployed old people and the starving children, whose corpses were collected daily from the streets and taken to the cemetery in large carts.

69

Jewish Cemetery, Warsaw

But what is to be done with the Jews? Do you think that in *Ostland* they will be accommodated in resettlement camps? ''What's all the fuss about?'' they asked us in Berlin. ''We cannot do anything with them in *Ostland* or in the *Reichkommissariat* either. Liquidate them yourselves.'' Gentlemen, I must ask you to rid yourselves of any feeling of pity . . . Ideas held up till now cannot be applied to such gigantic, unprecedented events. However, we must find a way to achieve the objective . . . We cannot shoot these 3,500,000 Jews. We cannot poison them. We shall, however, be able to take measures that will somehow lead to their eventual extermination.

Generalgouverneur Hans Frank

Theresienstadt Crematorium

In the Theresienstadt Ghetto camp near Prague, the transit station of many German Jews on the road to the gas chambers of Auschwitz, still existed cardboard urns for the ashes of the dead. In Warsaw, where in summer 1941, 5000 people perished every month, the corpses of those who had died from starvation were thrown by the hundred into mass graves. Only the rich could afford coffins.

According to the estimates of a jewish Medical Commission in the Warsaw Ghetto, the original plan to starve people to death would have taken five years. In summer 1942, when the techniques of mass murder had been sufficiently developed, the great transportations to the extermination camps began.

Bread for Bait

In accordance with our agreement, I have delivered to the Jewish Council of Elders: 6 pkts. rolled oats at 0·25 kg., 25 pkts. biscuits, 10 in each, 2 cases of jam—20 kg.

Due to lengthy storage and damage by mice, the food has become unfit for distribution by the rationing authorities.

Please pay into Court the cost price under Ref. 34 es 109/42.

Police to the Litzmannstadt Ghetto Administration, 8th January 1943

In accordance with the Order issued by the Authorities on 22nd July 1942, all persons not employed in institutions and enterprises will be evacuated. This compulsory evacuation will be carried out continuously.

Once again, I urge those subject to evacuation to report voluntarily at the *Umschlagplatz* and I extend for a further three days, i.e. 2nd, 3rd and 4th August 1942, *the issue of 3 kg. of bread and 1 kg. of jam to each volunteer.*
Families who report voluntarily *will not be separated.*

Appeal by the Warsaw Jewish Police, 1st August 1942

Before Deportation

The Germans forced the Jews from one corner to another, lashing out with whips and shooting. People were trampling on each other. Many of them started to say the Prayer for the Dying.

I lost Mummy. Her hand was torn from mine by the crowd. I bit and kicked. I defended myself because they were pushing me, but nobody took any notice. Everyone could see death before their eyes. I fell down, was trampled on. I thought I was going to die too. Somebody picked me up in his arms and cried: ''Save the child!''

Rebecca Kleiner, eight years old

74

Jewish "Civil Police" in Action

1. Fròm 5.9.1942 onwards an evacuation of Jews will be carried out in Sanok.
2. Any person who jeopardises or obstructs the evacuation in any way whatsoever, or assists in such activity, is to be shot.
3. Any person who shelters or hides a Jew during the course of or following the evacuation is to be shot.
4. Any person who enters the premises of an evacuated Jew without authorisation is to be shot as a looter.
5. During the course of the evacuation loitering in the streets is forbidden and windows are to remain closed.

Announcement of the Chief of the SS and Police in the District of Crackow, 4th September 1942

I arranged a meeting with *Hauptsturmfuehrer* Hoefle for Monday, 16.3.42, at 17.30 hours. During the course of the meeting, *Hauptsturmfuehrer* Hoefle stated:

1. It would be convenient if the transports of Jews arriving in the District of Lublin were divided at their station of departure into those able to work and those unable to work. If this was not possible at the station of departure, the segregation from the above point of view might possibly be done in Lublin.
2. Jews not capable of utilisation as labour were to come to Belsec, the outer frontier station in the Zamosc District . . . Finally, he stated that he could accept four to five transports of 1000 Jews each per day, destination Belsec (!).

Signature illegible

The evacuation of old, weak and ailing persons over the age of 65 years, of sick and ailing persons irrespective of age, as well as children under the age of 10, was scheduled to begin on 7.9.1942. Without warning whole blocks were cordonned off by the Evacuation Authorities (Gestapo) assisted by the Jewish Police. The evacuation lasted until 12.9.1942 inclusive. It dealt with about 18,000 persons, adults and children.

Litzmannstadt Ghetto Commissariat to the Chief of the Security Police, 24th September 1942

Evacuation of the Sick in Lodz

"Umschlagplatz" in Warsaw *(right)*

Since 22.7, trains containing 5000 Jews each have been leaving Warsaw daily, going via Malkinia to Treblinka. In addition trains containing 5000 go twice a week from Przemysl to Belsec. The Eastern Railway Executive has been in constant touch with the Security Police in Crackow. They agree that the transports from Warsaw via Lublin to Sobibor (near Lublin) should be held in abeyance so long as the alterations on the line makes these transports impossible (approx. October 1942).

Under-Secretary of State Theodor Ganzenmueller, Reich Ministry of Transport, 28th July 1942

I learned with particular pleasure from your communication that a train containing 5000 members of the Chosen People has now been leaving for Treblinka every day for a fortnight . . . I have contacted the authorities concerned to ensure that the entire operation is carried out without a hitch.

Reply from SS Obergruppenfuehrer Karl Wolff, Himmler's Field Adjutant, 13th August 1942

The Last Journey

Beginning with Lublin, the Jews are being deported from the *Generalgouvernement* to the east. Here a somewhat barbaric procedure is employed, not to be described in detail, and there is not much left of the Jews themselves. Generally speaking, it may be said that 60 per cent of them must be liquidated, while only 40 per cent can be utilised as labour. The former *Gauleiter* of Vienna (Globocnik), who is carrying out this *Aktion*, is doing so with considerable circumspection, using a procedure that is not too conspicuous . . . As the ghettos in the towns of the *Generalgouvernement* become vacant, they are filled with Jews deported from the *Reich*, and here, after a certain lapse of time, the process shall be repeated.

Entry in the diary of Josef Goebbels, 27th March 1942

Mass Executions

On 22nd July 1941 Hitler invaded the Soviet Union. He was now master of Europe and his power seemed boundless. The Soviet Union was the last country into which his armies marched, but the first to be subjected immediately to the extermination programme. Here, where he was not held back by any diplomatic considerations whatsoever, the Security Police began with the barbaric wholesale slaughter of the Jewish population, a year before the great deportations from Western Europe to the Polish extermination camps took place.

The population could not always be evacuated to safety in time. Many Jews remained of their own volition against the advice of the Soviet authorities. The older ones among them still remembered the Germans of the First World War, and were not afraid. They did not know what had become of Germany in the intervening period.

In every Russian village captured by the German troops, the Special Action Squads organised bloody massacres in a matter of days. In some places, where the army needed a particular labour force for a certain time, ghettos were introduced as a temporary measure. In most cases, however, people were simply driven to an embankment or anti-tank ditch outside the town and killed on the spot.

"Just allocation of labour. Only resettlement," the Germans would tell them, so that they would climb unprotesting into the lorries that took them to the place of execution. Once in the trap, they were driven out of the lorries with whips. Surrounded by guns and steel helmets and before the open pits containing the corpses of their neighbours who had left only half an hour before them, most of them saw no way out. Speechless with horror and paralysed with the fear of death, their only wish was to get it over as quickly as possible before they were maltreated still further. How could they have defended themselves in any case, naked as they were and faced with heavily armed killers?

And who would wish to leave his aged parents, his wife, his children, who could not escape, alone in their hour of death? Young people, who no longer had families, did sometimes, with the courage born of despair, attempt a last-minute flight. A very few escaped. Almost a million, however, remained in the pits.

The further the *Wehrmacht* advanced eastwards, the greater was the field of activity of the firing-squads. Four Special Action Squads combed the occupied territory of the Soviet Union from the Baltic to the Caucasus. As everywhere else, the worst elements from the native population were put to use, and auxiliary troops were formed with Lithuanian and Ukrainian volunteers. As the executions were officially described as the fight against partisans, military police and the *Wehrmacht* also took some part in these operations.

Often soldiers who had incurred some penalty were forced to serve their term of probation in the Special Action Squads. Many of them suffered nervous breakdowns or took their own lives. Others volunteered, attracted by the prospect of triple pay, three-monthly leave, special issues of *Schnaps* and opportunities for looting.

Like all murderers, the Nazis tried to cover the traces of their crime. After the Battle of Stalingrad the *"Kommando 1005"* was put into action, a brigade of Jewish prisoners, who had the ghastly task of re-opening the enormous mass graves and disposing of the rotting bodies.

A man who escaped has described how they had to stack up the human bodies into a mountainous funeral pile, burn them, break up the remains of the bones, sift the earth, sew grass and scatter the ashes to the winds. The number of mass graves was too large, however, and the Soviet advance was too rapid. So in the liberated territory, huge Golgothas were found everywhere.

In 1944, 18 months after the beginning of the big counter-offensive, Russian soldiers in Odessa encountered surviving Jews for the first time.

Three Reports

Immediately following military action, the Jewish population remained temporarily unmolested. Not until some weeks, sometimes months, later was systematic execution of the Jews carried out by police units formed for the purpose. In the main, this *Aktion* proceeded from east to west. It always took place publicly with the co-operation of Ukrainian militia and, more regrettably, with voluntary participation by members of the *Wehrmacht*. The way in which these operations, which included young and old men, women and children of all ages, were carried out was horrible. The mass scale of the executions make this *Aktion* more colossal than any similar measures undertaken in the Soviet Union so far. Altogether some 150,000 to 200,000 Jews in the part of the Ukraine belonging to the *Reichskommissariat* may have been executed up till now . . .

Report of an Armaments Inspector in the Ukraine, 2nd December 1941

The systematic cleansing work in *Ostland*, in accordance with basic orders, includes the complete as possible elimination of Jewry. This objective, with the exception of White Ruthenia, has on the whole been reached by the execution of 229,052 Jews so far (see enclosure). The remainder, in the Baltic Provinces, is urgently needed as labour and is accommodated in ghettos . . .

The final and fundamental elimination of Jews remaining in White Ruthenia after the invasion by the Germans incurs certain difficulties. Here Jewry forms an unusually high percentage of the skilled workers, who are, due to a shortage of other reserves, indispensable in that region.

Furthermore, *Einsatzgruppe A* took over the district after the onset of heavy frost, which made the mass executions very much more difficult. A further difficulty consists in the fact that the Jews are widely dispersed over the whole countryside. The long distances, difficult communications, the shortage of motor vehicles and petrol, and the limited resources of the Security Police make the executions in the countryside possible only by stretching resources to the utmost. Nevertheless, 41,000 Jews have been executed so far . . . About 18,000 Jews—excluding *Reich* Germans—live at the moment in Minsk itself. Their execution has had to be postponed due to consideration of the labour supply.

The Commanding Officer in White Ruthenia is instructed, despite the difficult conditions, to settle the Jewish question as soon as possible. A period of about a further two months—depending on weather conditions—will be necessary.

Secret Progress Report of Einsatzgruppe A, February 1942

After thorough consultation with *SS-Brigadefuehrer* Zenner and the outstandingly able leader of the SD, *SS-Obersturmbannfuehrer* Dr. jur. Strauch, we have liquidated about 55,000 Jews in White Ruthenia in the last ten weeks. In the region of Minsk, Jewry has been completely wiped out, without jeopardising the labour situation. In the predominantly Polish region of Lida, 16,000 Jews, in Slonim 8000 Jews, etc., have been liquidated . . .

The rear army has, without contact with myself, liquidated 10,000 Jews, who we had in any case intended to wipe out systematically. In the town of Minsk, on 28th and 29th July, about 10,000 Jews were liquidated, including 6500 Russian Jews—predominantly old people, women and children—the rest consisted of Jews unfit for utilisation as labour, most of whom had been sent on orders of the *Fuehrer* from Vienna, Brunn, Bremen and Berlin in November of last year.

The region of Sluzk is also lighter by several thousand Jews. The same applies to Novogrodek and Vileyka. Radical measures have still to be taken in Baranovichi and Hantsevichi. In Baranovichi about 10,000 Jews still live in the town alone, of whom 9000 will be liquidated next month . . .

In addition to this uncompromising attitude vis-à-vis Jewry, the SD in White Ruthenia have the difficult task of ensuring that the new transports of Jews, continuously arriving from the *Reich*, reach their destination.

Report of Wilhelm Kube, Generalkommissar for White Ruthenia, 31st July 1942

I saw it happen   *The execution of the Jews in Dubno*

From September 1941 until January 1944, I was general manager and chief engineer of a branch office of the construction company Josef Jung, Solingen, located in Sdolbunow, Ukraine. In this capacity I had to inspect the construction sites of my company. For an army construction depot my company was building warehouses for grain storage on the former airstrip near Dubno, Ukraine.

On 5th October 1942, when I visited the building office at Dubno, my foreman, Hubert Moennikes, told me that in the vicinity of the site Jews from Dubno had been shot in three large pits, each about 30 m. long and 3 m. deep. About 1500 persons had been killed daily. All of the 5000 Jews who had still been living in Dubno before the pogrom were to be liquidated. As the shooting had taken place in his presence he was still very upset...

Moennikes and I went straight to the pits. Nobody prevented us. I heard a quick succession of shots from behind one of the mounds of earth. The people who had got off the lorries—men, women and children of all ages—had to undress upon the order of an SS man, who carried a riding or dog whip. They had to put their clothes on separate piles of shoes, top clothing and underclothing. I saw a heap of shoes that must have contained 800 to 1000 pairs, great piles of clothes and under-garments. Without screaming or weeping these people undressed, stood in family groups, kissed each other, said their farewells, and waited for a sign from another SS man, who stood near the pit, also with a whip in his hand. During the fifteen minutes that I stood near the pit, I did not hear any-one complain or beg for mercy.

I watched a family of about eight, a man and a woman, both about 50, with their children, aged about one, eight and ten, and two grown-up daughters of about 20 to 24. An old woman with snow-white hair was holding the one-year-old child in her arms, singing something to it and tickling it. The child was crowing with delight. The man and wife were looking on with tears in their eyes. The father was holding the hand of a boy of about ten, speaking to him softly. The boy was fighting back his tears. The father pointed to the sky, stroked the boy's head and seemed to explain some-thing to him. At that moment the SS man at the pit shouted something to his comrade, who separated off about 20 persons and ordered them to go behind the mound of earth. Among them was the family that I have mentioned. I still clearly remember a dark-haired, slim girl who pointed to herself as she passed close to me and said ''Twenty-three''.

I walked to the other side of the mound and found myself standing before an enormous grave. The people lay so closely packed, one on top of the other, that only their heads were visible. Nearly all had blood running over their shoulders from their heads. Some of them were still moving. Some lifted an arm and turned a head to show that they were still alive. The pit was already two-thirds full. I estimated that it already contained about 1000 people. I looked round for the man who had shot them. He was an SS man, who was sitting on the edge of the narrow end of the pit, his legs dangling into it. He had a sub-machine gun across his knees and was smoking a cigarette. The people, completely naked, went down some steps which had been cut in the clay wall of the pit and climbed over the heads of those already lying there, to the place indicated by the SS man. They laid down in front of the dead or injured people. Some of them caressed those who were still alive and spoke to them softly. Then I heard a series of shots. I looked into the pit and saw that the bodies were twitching or that the heads lay motionless on top of the bodies which lay before them. Blood was pouring from their necks. I was surprised that I was not ordered away, but saw that there were also two or three uniformed postmen standing nearby. The next batch was already approaching. They climbed into the pit, lined up against the previous victims and were shot. When I walked back round the mound I noticed another lorry-load of people which had just arrived. This time it included sick and infirm people. A very thin old woman, with terribly thin legs, was undressed by others who were already naked, while two people supported her. The woman appeared to be paralysed. The naked people carried the woman around the mound. I left with Moennikes and drove back to Dubno in the car.

Affidavit of Construction Engineer Hermann Friedrich Graebe in Wiesbaden, 10th November 1945

I took part *The execution of the Jews in Shirowitz*

In 1941 I was called up for service with the Rosenberg *Einsatz* staff and was assigned to the district *Kommissar* of Slonim as an interpreter. I also served as a driver. I was in Slonim from July 1941 until 15th December 1943.

...Shirowitz is on the outskirts of Slonim and about 7—9 km. away. At this execution about 1200 to 1400 Jews from the ghetto were exterminated. In this *Aktion* groups of 500 persons were led on foot to the place of extermination and exterminated by the detailed extermination units. I was myself present at this execution and myself took part in the shooting. The pits were this time 4 m. wide, 5 m. deep and about 60—80 m. long. The place of execution was outside the village behind a small wood. A few days before the execution firing tests were carried out at the place of execution to find out whether the inhabitants of Shirowitz could hear the sound of the executions.

The execution proceeded roughly as follows: the guards went into the pits with the Jews. In this way the rear end of the pits was closed off and the Jews forced to undress on the edge and to lie down immediately in the pits without a search. When the first batch was lying inside, the guards came out of the pits while simultaneous fire took place from both sides. By this type of arrangement it was possible to open a cross-fire on the Jews. The first batch amounted to about 100—120 persons in the pit. After the first execution the second batch had to lie down on the dead bodies in such a way that the head lay on the feet of the corpses underneath. In one pit about 5—6 batches were thrown in on top of one another and the total of Jews in one pit was about 400—500 persons. The execution was carried out with quick-firing guns, carbines and sub-machine guns completely at our discretion. Previously many were beaten to death. It was amazing how the Jews went down into the pits, only exchanging mutual words of comfort, to encourage each other and make the work of the Execution Units easier. The execution itself lasted 3—4 hours. I took part in the execution the whole time. The only pauses that I made was when my carbine was empty and I had to re-load. It is therefore not possible for me to say how many Jews I myself killed in these 3—4 hours as during this time someone else shot in my place. During this time we drank quite a lot of *Schnaps* to stimulate our zeal for work. The Jews in the lower batches who were alive or only wounded were suffocated by the upper batches or drowned in the blood of the upper batches. This time no wounded people came out alive. The graves were then filled in by local inhabitants. After this mass extermination another meeting with the District *Kommissar* was held. The District *Kommissar* took the opportunity to praise my diligence and was satisfied with the whole *Aktion* ...

III. In this way further executions in other villages were carried out, in Koslovchisna, about 700—800 Jews, in Berechin about 2000—3000 persons, in Holinka 400—500 Jews, in Bytin about 3000—4000. All those who were present at the previous execution had to take part again in these executions. We used the same weapons. In addition, Mr. Muck, NCO, and soldiers and railway workers from Slonim Station took part voluntarily once they saw that there was something to be gained from the executions. In these executions clothes and pieces of jewellery were taken off before the execution. Physical searches did not take place due to lack of time.

IV. In one of these villages there was a resistance organisation which was discovered by the Security Police. The people were interrogated particularly closely and maltreated and subsequently shot with the Jews. There were 80 Poles from the National Congress. The leader of these Security Police units was *SS-Untersturmfuehrer* Amelung. I also took part in this execution ...

V. The second extermination in Slonim was in autumn 1943 and was to have been the ultimate solution of the Jewish problem in this locality. This settlement was ordered for all the Commisariats, and the first District *Kommissar* to settle the Jewish problem was to have been subsequently promoted. I should like to mention in addition that 85 per cent of the population were Jews. In 18 months, 24,000 Jews were exterminated in this district.

Affidavit of Alfred Metzner, interpreter, in Augsburg, 18th September 1947

"Aktion" in Wlodawa, October 1942

Jews digging their own Grave *(pages 86–87)*

The excavation of the pits takes up most of the time, whereas the execution itself is very quick (100 persons takes 40 minutes) . . . At first my men were not affected. On the second day, however, it was already apparent that one or two did not have the nerves to carry out executions over a period. My personal impression is that during the execution one does not have any scruples. These make themselves felt, however, days later when one is quietly thinking about it in the evening.

Report of Oberleutnant Walther on an execution near Belgrade on 1st November 1941

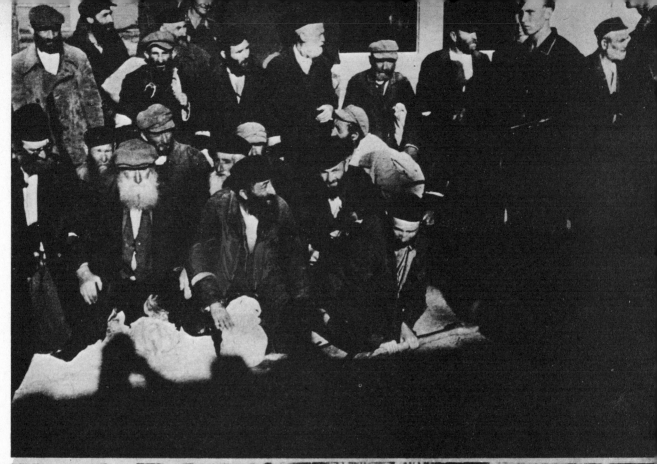

Poland

We are having a proper clear-out of course, especially among the Jews... We are not asleep here. Three or four *Aktionen* a week. Once gipsies and another time Jews, partisans and other riff-raff... Well, of the 24,000 Yids we had here in Kamieniec-Podolsk only a tiny percentage is still alive. The Yids living in the district are likewise among our select clientele. We are pressing on without pangs of conscience, and then: ''...the waves cover them up, the world is at peace.''

Gendarmeriemeister Fritz Jacob to Generalleutnant Querner, 21st June 1942

Registration in Odessa on 22nd October 1941

Official use only! Propaganda company 649, Archives no. 23/27. Photographer: Sommerschuh, Text: Schoner. Place: Odessa, Date: 22.10.41.

Text: Criminal elements in their proper place.

Jews from Odessa, who had to report in the prison yard after the fall of the city. They were all registered and will soon get the opportunity for physical work, because their parasitic existence in Soviet-Judea has now come to an end for them.

Official text on the reverse of the photographs below.

The enemy has been provided with propaganda material that is more effective than anything that could have been thought up anywhere in the whole world. What the foreign stations have broadcast so far is only a tiny fraction of what has actually taken place. The outcry from abroad can be expected to grow steadily and cause the greatest political damage, especially as the atrocities have in fact taken place and cannot be refuted by anything.

92

Generaloberst Blaskowitz

Sniadowa, Poland

"The Jewish race is being exterminated," every party member says, "that's quite clear, it's in our programme. Elimination of the Jews, and we're doing it." Not one of all those who talk like this has witnessed it, not one has been through it. Most of you will know what it means when 100 corpses are lying side by side, when 500 are lying there or when 1000 are lying there. To have stuck this out and at the same time—apart from exceptions due to human weaknesses—to have remained decent, that is what has made us hard. This is a page of glory in our history which has never been written and is never to be written.

Heinrich Himmler

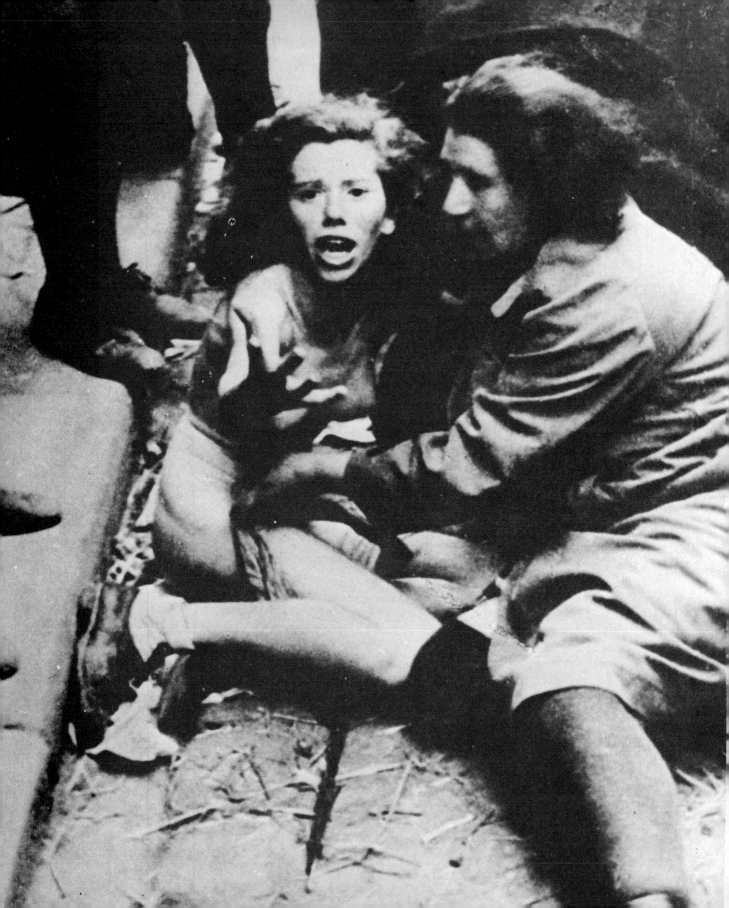

We realise that it is now pointless to discuss the various proposals for the solution; the Jewish question has passed from the theoretical to the purely practical stage and, indeed, not just in Germany, but on an increasing scale in the other European countries . . . The fate of the Jews is now unfolding in accordance with the laws of a justice that cares nothing for petty sensibilities and that incorruptibly serves the good of humanity. The verdict on the Jews in Europe has been spoken.

"Die Front", army field newspaper, No. 414, 18th July 1942

Manhunt in Lvov and Lijepaja

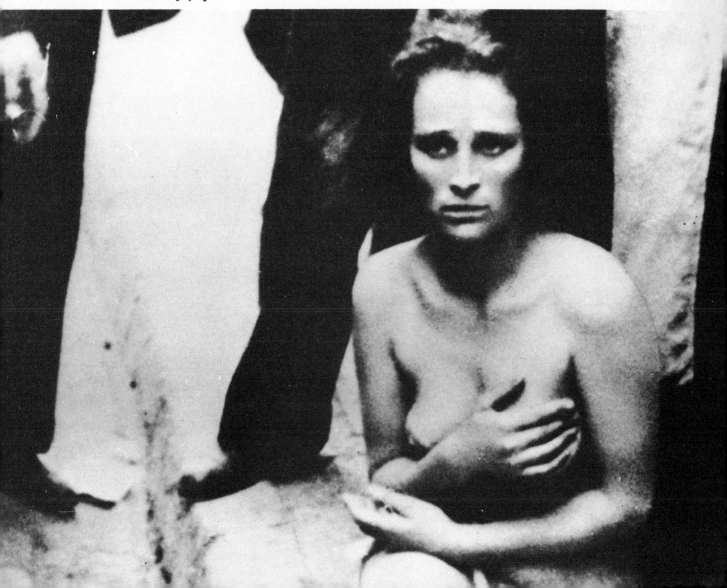

Mass executions in Lijepaja, Latvia

Before shooting them, the executioners forced their victims to take off their clothes and shoes. Accounts were kept of the money, jewellery and watches collected in bucketfuls by the guards.

Among the *Gestapo* documents found in the town of Lijepaja in Latvia after the retreat of the German troops was the series of photographs of a mass execution published here.

What is Katyn against this? Just imagine that these events were to become known to the enemy and were being exploited by them! In all probability such propaganda would be ineffective simply because those hearing and reading it would not be prepared to believe it.

The Reichskommissar for the Ostland to the Reichsminister for the occupied Eastern Territories, 18th June 1943

Execution of Jewish Hostages in Dragobich, USSR *(above right)*

Execution of Resistance Fighters, USSR *(below right)*

This girl is one of the few whose picture and name the killers left behind. Baila Gelblung escaped from a death train from the Warsaw Ghetto and joined the partisans. When she was arrested in Brest-Litovsk, she was wearing a Polish military jacket. This photograph of her interrogation appeared during the war in a German illustrated paper.

100   We do not know the names of these two Russians and we do not know why they had to die. Perhaps they hid an escaped Jew, perhaps they helped the partisans. Their young faces, in the very minute of death, stand for hundreds of thousands who were executed for supporting the cause of the persecuted against the persecutors.

The Deportations

The conquests in the West presented the extermination fanatics with new problems. For a time they toyed with the abstruse idea of banishing all European Jews to the island of Madagascar and of leaving them to their fate. The project was soon dropped, however.

A month after the invasion of the Soviet Union, Goering charged Reinhard Heydrich, the Chief of the Security Police, with the organisational preparations for the "final solution of the Jewish problem" in the German-occupied territories. Six months later, the completed plans were submitted.

On 20th January 1942, when the wholesale executions were already well under way, the deportations from the German *Reich* had begun and in Poland the first people were being driven into the gas chambers, Heydrich called a meeting "to be followed by breakfast". At a conference in the Berlin suburb of Wannsee, he informed representatives from the relevant Ministries of the forthcoming operations in order to secure their co-operation.

In the Spring of the same year, the great manhunt began. The same tragedy was repeated in all the occupied countries. It had started with registration, the introduction of the Jewish Star insignia and the passing of anti-Semitic laws. Now the deportations began.

Everything was controlled by regulations and proceeded strictly according to plan. Instructions were issued as to how much each person could take with them: food for two days, a bowl, no knife, a spoon, two blankets, warm clothing, a pair of stout shoes—maximum weight 55 lb— and a suitcase, on which the owner had to write his name and which he would never open again. In the street a lorry full of people would be waiting to drive to the transit camp or direct to the goods station. A train waited at the platform. It had twenty cattle wagons with barbed wire nailed over the windows, and two passenger coaches for the guards. Such a transport accommodated a thousand persons.

The trains went several times a week to and from all the stations of Europe. Even the shortage of supplies urgently needed for the front and the obstruction of the lines of withdrawal did not prevent the German Government from carrying out its programme.

A farewell, a last look, an embrace. Thousands, hundreds of thousands, millions of times. Families split up, friends parted. A man, with his private hopes and fears, repeated a thousandfold. A whole life stolen: a name wiped out.

For several days and nights they huddled among their baggage in the half-light of the over-crowded cattle wagons. They were haggard from lack of sleep, thirsty and in despair, ignorant of their destination. The bottle of water was soon empty: the waste bin overflowed. The children cried, women fainted. On the second morning they would discover their first dead—a baby who could not withstand the hardships of the journey, an old man whose heart had failed him.

Sometimes, when the train stopped at a German station, the deportees saw Red Cross nurses giving out coffee to soldiers who were passing through. For Jews in Germany, however, there was not even water.

To make it easier to round them up, the victims were told that they were going to work in Poland. As the truth filtered through, people tried with increasing desperation to hide somewhere— with a forged identity card, in a village where nobody knew them, or in hiding, in the attic of someone brave enough to help. Any person not going to the collection point voluntarily would be fetched. Frequently the police would come to a deserted house. Frequently they had to break down the doors because those they had come to collect could no longer hear the bell.

A modern migration of peoples had begun. From Oslo and Athens, Paris and Amsterdam, Berlin and Prague, Vienna and Budapest, streamed the unending processions towards one place of which nobody had heard before—Auschwitz.

A terrible fate had overtaken the Children of Israel. But this fate had name, address, face: Dept. IV B, SS-Obersturmbannfuehrer Adolf Eichmann, Central Security Office of the State, Berlin.

Gemeente 's-Gravenhage

AANMELDINGSPLICHT

van personen van geheel of gedeeltelijk Joodschen bloede.

Сви Јевреји морају да се пријаве 19 априла т. г. у 8 час. у јутро градској полицији (у згради Пожарне команде на Ташмајдану).

Јевреји који се не одазову овом позиву биће стрељани.

Београд, 16-IV-1911 год.

Шеф групе полиције безбедности и С. Д.

ETAT FRANCAIS

Ville de VICHY

ARRETE MUNICIPAL

RECENSEMENT des ISRAELITES

The "Final Solution" Order

The Reich Marshal of the Greater German Reich   Berlin, 31.7.1941
Commissioner for the Four-Year Plan
Chairman of the Ministerial Council for National Defence

To the Chief of the Security Police and the Security Service
—*Gruppenfuehrer* Heydrich—Berlin

Complementing the task that was assigned to you on 24th January 1939, of arriving at, by means of emigration and evacuation, as favourable a solution as possible in the circumstances obtaining at the time, I hereby charge you with making all the requisite organisational, technical and material preparations for a complete solution of the Jewish question in the German sphere of influence in Europe.

In so far as the competence of other government agencies are thereby affected, these are to co-operate.

I charge you further to submit to me in the near future an over-all plan of the preliminary organisational, technical and material measures for the accomplishment of the desired final solution of the Jewish question.

Goering

"Secret Affair of State" *Transcript of the Wannsee Conference of 20th January 1942*

Following previous approval by the *Fuehrer*, evacuation to the East has now replaced emigration as a further possible solution.

These measures are to be regarded merely as possible alternatives, but practical experience is already being gained here that is of great importance with regard to the coming final solution of the Jewish question.

In the course of this final solution of the European Jewish question about 11 million Jews come under consideration . . . In the course of the final solution the Jews must be mobilised for labour in the East in a suitable manner under appropriate direction. In large colonies, with separation of the sexes, the Jews who are capable of work will be directed in road-building in this territory, during which no doubt a large proportion will be eliminated by a process of natural reduction.

The eventual remainder that is finally left will, as this will doubtless be the most resistant element, be suitably dealt with as this, constituting the result of natural selection, is to be regarded as the nucleus of a Jewish revival if set at liberty. (See the lessons of history.)

In the course of the practical execution of the final solution Europe will be combed from west to east. The territory of the *Reich*, including Bohemia and Moravia, for reasons of the housing problem and other social and political requirements, will have to be given precedence. The evacuated Jews will first be transferred continuously to the so-called transit ghettos, to be transported from there to the East . . .

The start of the individual large-scale evacuations will depend to a large extent on the military situation. With respect to the handling of the final solution in the European territories occupied or influenced by us, it was suggested that the Foreign Office official specialists concerned discuss this with the competent special advisors of the *Sicherheitspolizei* and the SD . . . Finally, a discussion took place on the various possible methods of bringing about the solution, during which *Gauleiter* Dr. Mayer and Secretary of State Dr. Buehler took the point of view that certain preparatory work should be carried out in the respective territories themselves, avoiding, however, arousing alarm among the population. With the request of the Chief of the *Sicherheitspolizei* and the SD to the participants in the conference that they give him suitable support in the execution of the tasks involved in the solution, the conference was closed.

Guiding Principles for the Deportations

Geheime Staatspolizei   Bielefeld, 20th March 1942
Muenster Police Station—Bielefeld Field Duty Station—

Ref: No. II B 3—944/42

To the District President—Chief Burgomaster
in . . . .

Re: Evacuation of Jews
Previous Corresp.: None
Encls.: 1 list of names, receipt forms, copies of this order

On 31.3.42, 1000 Jews will be evacuated to the East from the district of the Hanover Main Police Station. The evacuation of 325 Jews from the former district of the Bielefeld Main Police Station (Minden and Lippe and Schaumburg-Lippe) is to be arranged. The names of Jews to be evacuated from the individual police sub-districts are entered on the attached list. The sub-district police authorities are to effect the following:

1. The Jews due for deportation are to be fetched from their homes on 30.3.42 and by noon of the same day *at the latest* are to be conveyed to Bielefeld to the Large Hall of the *Kyffhaeuser* (Kesselbrink). The executive officers acting as escort are to undertake the transportation in civilian clothes. As far as possible the transports are to take place by train.
2. Before the Jews leave the premises, an official must collect in all ready cash, valuables (jewellery, gold and silver articles, including gold watches)—excluding wedding rings. On the premises of the Jew concerned, one of the enclosed receipts is then to be made out by an official, and signed by two officials and the Jew concerned, whose belongings have been taken into safe keeping. The cash and valuables are then to be *sealed* with the receipt under the same cover and handed over to the police officer supervising at the reception depot in Bielefeld (*Kyffhaeuser*).
3. Before leaving the Jewish premises, it must be made sure that the gas and water are turned off and the light is switched off (black-out!).
4. Immediately after leaving the premises, they are to be sealed. Sealing stamps are to be used for this purposes. The keys to the premises are to be collected in by the local police and deposited at the station. They are to be tied together and attached to a label on which the name and address of the Jew is written . . .
5. Upon delivery at the reception depot the Jews must be in possession only of their identity cards. All other papers are to be left behind in their dwellings. Ration cards are to be withdrawn and sent to the appropriate food office. Employment record books and pension cards are likewise to be withdrawn and sent to the appropriate labour exchange or pension insurance office.
6. The Jews due for evacuation are instructed to take 25 kg. of baggage. In addition, food for two days may be taken. The local police authorities have to collect the baggage of the Jews on 28.3.42 and keep it until departure. Before the evacuation starts, the baggage is to be *reweighed and examined meticulously*. The baggage may not contain any weapons (fire-arms, explosives, knives, scissors, poison, medicine, etc.). If the baggage is heavier than 25 kg. it is to be reduced accordingly. The Jews are also to be instructed that they may take with them up to two blankets which, however, must be included in the 25 kg. . . .

I particularly draw your attention to the fact that the above orders, which are laid down in accordance with the guiding principles issued by the Central Security Office of the State, are to be carried out exactly.

He.

The Story of a Deportation

"Report on the evacuation of Jews to Riga"

Progress of the transport. The transport of Jews scheduled for 11.12.1941 includes 1007 Jews from the towns of Duisburg, Krefeld, several smaller towns and rural communities of the Rhine-Westphalian industrial district. Dusseldorf was represented by only 19 Jews. The transport was composed of Jews of both sexes and various ages, from babies up to the age of 65.

The departure of the transport was scheduled for 9.30 hours. The Jews were therefore assembled on the platform by 4.00 hours in readiness for loading. The railway, however, reportedly due to manpower shortage, could not assemble the special train so early, so the loading of the Jews could not be started before about 9.00 hours. Because the railway urged that the train should leave as nearly as possible according to schedule, the loading was undertaken with the greatest haste . . .

On the way from the slaughter-house to the platform, a male Jew had attempted to commit suicide by throwing himself under a tram. He was caught on the tray of the tram, however, and only slightly injured. At first he pretended to be dying, but became very lively during the journey once he realised that he could not avoid the fate of evacuation.

Similarly, an elderly Jewess had left the platform unnoticed—it was raining and very dark— taken refuge in a nearby house, taken off her clothes and sat down in a toilet. She was discovered by a woman cleaner, however, so that she could be brought back to the transport. The loading of the Jews was completed at about 10.15 hours. After shunting several times the train then left the goods station of Dusseldorf-Derendorf at about 10.30 in the direction of Wuppertal . . .

The journey then went according to plan and the train passed through the following towns: Wuppertal, Hagen, Schwerte, Hamm. At about 18.00 hours Hannover-Linden was reached . . . At 3.30 hours the train stopped for half an hour at Berlin-Lichterfelde . . . The train was already 155 minutes behind schedule. The journey was continued via Kuestrin, Kreuz, Schneidemuehl, Firchau . . .

Just outside Konitz the train broke up because of overloading. A heating pipe was also broken. Improvised repairs were carried out and the train was able to continue its journey to Konitz . . . At 12.10 hours the train left Konitz. The journey then continued via Dirschau, Marienburg, Elbing to Koenigsberg (Pr.) . . . At 1.50 hours it went on to Tilsit . . . At 5.15 hours the frontier-station of Laugszargen and, 15 minutes later, the Lithuanian station of Tauroggen were reached. From there onwards the journey to Riga should normally have taken only another 14 hours. As a result of the single-line track and the train's secondary importance in dispatch, there were often long delays at the stations before the train could continue its journey. At Schaulen Station (1.12 hours), the escort personnel were catered for adequately and well by Red Cross nurses. Barley soup with beef was served . . . At 19.30 hours Mitau (Latvia) was reached. Here a considerable drop in the temperature was noticeable. It started to snow and frost followed. The arrival in Riga took place at 21.50 hours, where the train was detained in the station for $1\frac{1}{2}$ hours. Here I ascertained that the Jews were not destined for the Riga Ghetto but were to be accommodated in the Stirotawa Ghetto, 8 km. north-east of Riga. On 13.12, at 23.35 hours, the train, after much shunting up and down the line, reached the military platform on Stirotawa Station. The train remained standing, without heating. The temperature outside was already 12 deg. below zero. As the police detachment who were to take command were not present, my men continued to guard the train. The handing-over of the train took place at 1.45 hours, when the guard was taken over by six Latvian policemen. As it was already after midnight, it was dark and the platform was heavily iced over, the unloading and conveying of the Jews to the assembly ghetto 2km. away could not take place before early on Sunday when it got light. My escort party was taken to Riga in two police patrol cars made available by the police detachment, and given over-night accommodation at about 3.00 hours. I myself received shelter in the guest house of the Higher SS and Police Chief, Petersburger Hof, Am Schlossplatz 4.

signed: Salitter, Captain of the Schutzpolizei

The Example of Holland

"Re: Evacuation of the Jews"—*Consul-General Otto Bene, the representative of the Foreign Ministry to the Reichskommissar for the occupied Dutch Territories in the Hague, reports to Berlin*:

31st July 1942. With the trains that went today, 6000 Dutch Jews have been deported so far. The evacuation as such went off smoothly and it is to be expected that the transports leaving in the coming weeks will proceed without difficulties or hindrance.

13th August 1942. Since my report, mentioned above, the position has changed considerably. Now the Jews have found out what lies behind the evacuation and the mobilisation of labour in the East, they no longer report for the weekly transports. Out of the 2000 called up for this week, only about 400 appeared. They are not to be found in their homes. This makes it difficult, therefore, to fill the two trains and it is not yet known how the trains are to be filled in the coming weeks.

11th September 1942. It is estimated that about 25,000 Jews in the Netherlands are leading an ambulant existence, i.e. are in hiding. The evacuation figures have not been met so far. Various measures are in preparation to guarantee these figures in future.

16th November 1942. Since my report dated 11th September 1942—D Pol 3 No. 8—the evacuation of the Jews to Auschwitz Camp has proceeded without difficulties or incidents. By 15th October approx. 45,000 Jews were evacuated.

   The *Reichskommissar* has ordered that all Jews must be evacuated by 1st May 1943. This means that the weekly evacuation figure has had to be increased from 2000 to 3500.

6th January 1943. The evacuation of the Jews from the Netherlands has been proceeding smoothly since my report of 16.11.1942—D Pol 3 No. 8/No. 1558—with the result that a half of the Jews due for evacuation have now been deported.

26th March 1943. The following case shows how readily the Dutch still commit the offence of aiding and abetting Jews, either out of pity or avarice. Eight Aryans laid themselves open to prosecution on account of *one* Jew, whom they had supported and hidden among themselves for weeks . . . Even with the Dutch police escaping Jews are mainly brought in only by individual officials who have already been working for the German police for some time. The majority of police officials, due to fear of their superiors, comrades and the population, do not intervene.

30th April 1943. Various provincial authorities have reported suicides by Jews. The population, apart from friends made by mixed marriages, did not show any interest in the transports of Jews and seem to have become resigned to them.

24th May 1943. The evacuations to the East were not disrupted by the strike disturbances and the deployment elsewhere of the police personnel. The sixty-thousandth Jew has been deported for labour mobilisation in the East . . . The catching of escaping Jews in Amsterdam and in the provinces continues, in some cases with the payment of head-money to Dutchmen.

25th June 1943. Out of the 140,000 full Jews originally registered in the Netherlands, the 100,000th has now been removed from the national body . . . A last great increase was achieved on Sunday, 20.6.1943, by a second large-scale *Aktion* in Amsterdam, when 5500 Jews were caught in a 24-hour seizure . . . There were no incidents. The Dutch population disapproves of the deportations, but seems to take an outwardly indifferent attitude.

The Children of Drancy

The arrest of stateless Jews in Paris will be undertaken by the French police in the period from 16.7 to 18.7.1942. It is to be expected that following the arrests about 4000 Jewish children will be left behind . . . I ask for an urgent ruling by teleprinter as to whether the children of the stateless Jews who are to be deported can be included from about the tenth transport onwards.

Teleprinter message from the SS-Hauptsturmfuehrer Dannecker, Paris, to the Reichssicherheitshauptamt, Berlin, 10th July 1942

On 20.7.1942 *SS-Obersturmbannfuehrer* Eichmann and *SS-Obersturmfuehrer* Nowak of the RSHA IV B 4 telephoned.

The question of the evacuation of children was discussed with *SS-Obersturmbannfuehrer* Eichmann. He decided that, as soon as evacuation to the *Generalgouvernement* becomes possible again, transports of children can go.

Dannecker's file note, 21st July 1942

The Jewish children accommodated in the Pithiviers and Beaune-la-Rolande camps can gradually be distributed among the scheduled transports to Auschwitz. Transports composed exclusively of children, however, are on no account (underlined) to be sent off.

Teleprinter message from the RSHA to the Chief of the Security Police, Paris, 13th August 1942

On 14.8.1942, at 8.55 hours, transport train No. D901/14 left the station of departure Le Bourget-Drancy for Auschwitz with a total of 1000 Jews. (Children among them for the first time.) The categories of persons caught correspond to the guiding principles that have been laid down . . .

Teleprinter message from SS-Obersturmfuehrer Roethke, Paris, to the RSHA, the Inspector of the Concentration Camps and the Auschwitz Concentration Camp, 14th August 1942

On the day of the deportation the children were usually woken at five o'clock in the morning and dressed in the half-light. It was often cold at five o'clock in the morning, but nearly all the children went down to the yard very lightly clad. Suddenly roused from sleep, ill with sleepiness, the littlest ones would begin to cry and, one by one, the others followed their example. They did not want to go down to the yard, struggled and would not let themselves be dressed. Sometimes it happened that a whole roomful of a hundred children, seized with panic and unconquerable terror, no longer responded to the comforting words of the adults who tried vainly to get them to go downstairs. Then the gendarmes were called, who carried the children down, screaming with terror.

In the yard they waited to be called: they often answered wrongly when their names were called out. The older ones held on to the little ones' hands and would not let go of them. There was a certain number of children in each transport added at the end: those whose names were unknown. These were entered on the list by a question mark. It was of no great importance: it was doubtful whether even the half of the unfortunate children would withstand the journey. There was no doubt at all that the survivors would be exterminated shortly after their arrival.

In this way 4000 children, who had been left behind by the evacuation of their parents, were deported in two weeks. This took place in the second half of the month of August 1942.

Report of Georges Wellers

The Protest of the Dutch Churches

The following points from a declaration from the pulpit, which was read out on Sunday, 26.7.1942, in all Dutch churches of *all* denominations, should be mentioned:

1. The Churches declare themselves called upon in the name of law and justice to *protest against the expulsion of Jews and against the deportation of workers to Germany.*

2. In the pulpit declaration they make known to the public a telegram that they sent to the *Reichskommissar* on 11th July. It runs as follows:

"The undersigned Dutch Churches, already deeply shocked by the measures against the Jews in the Netherlands, which exclude them from participation in the normal life of the people, were horrified to learn of the new measures under which men, women and children and entire families shall be deported to *Reich* territory and territories under *Reich* control. The suffering that this will inflict on tens of thousands, the knowledge that *these measures are repugnant to the deepest moral consciousness of the Dutch people* and, above all, the violation inherent in these measures of the law and justice laid down by God, compel the Churches to address to you the most urgent plea not to implement these measures. On behalf of the Christians among the Jews this urgent plea is enjoined on us by the additional consideration that by these measures they will be cut off from participation in the life of the Church.

> The Dutch Reformed Church
> The Archbishop and Bishops of the Roman Catholic Church in the Netherlands
> The Calvinist Churches in the Netherlands
> The General Mennonite Sect
> The Remonstrant Brotherhood
> The Old Reformed Church in the Netherlands
> The Reformed Sect in the Netherlands
> The Evangelist Lutheran Church in the Netherlands
> The New Evangelist Lutheran Church in the Kingdom of the Netherlands"

Report by Otto Bene, Consul-General in The Hague, to the Foreign Ministry in Berlin, 31st July 1942

The Attitude of the Vatican

The Pope, although he is said to be under pressure from various sides, *has not allowed himself to be forced into any demonstrative statement against the deportation of the Jews from Rome.* Although he can expect this attitude to be resented by our enemies and exploited by the Protestant circles in Anglo-Saxon countries for the purpose of propaganda against Catholicism, he has *done all he could in this delicate question to avoid straining relations with the German Government and the German authorities in Rome.* As here in Rome further German *Aktionen* in respect of the Jewish question are no longer likely to be carried out, *the matter, which is awkward from the point of view of German-Vatican relations, can therefore be regarded as settled.*

An indication of the Vatican attitude has in fact already appeared. The *Osservatore Romano* published in a prominent position on 25/26th October an official communiqué on the activity of apostolic love on the part of the Pope, which says, in the style characteristic of the Vatican newspaper, i.e., extremely tortuous and vague, that the Pope bestows his fatherly care on all men, irrespective of nationality *and race*. The many-sided and constant activity of Pius XII has increased recently as a result of the increased suffering of so many unfortunates.

There is all the less reason to raise objections to this announcement since the wording, a translation of which is attached, will be taken by few people as referring specifically to the Jewish question.

Letter by courier from Ernst von Weizsaecker, German Ambassador to the Holy See, to the Foreign Ministry, Berlin, 28th October 1943

Budapest,
Announcements

One of the most impressive demonstrations of resistance was the great solidarity strike by the Dutch workers on 25th and 26th February 1941.

During a police raid in Amsterdam's historic Jewish quarter a clash took place between Dutch collaborators and dockworkers who rushed to the aid of the harassed Jews. A policeman was wounded and died. His funeral, staged for propaganda purposes, led to renewed disturbances.

As a result, Himmler had 400 Jewish hostages arrested on 22nd February. These unfortunate young men, all between the ages of 20 and 35, were dragged from their homes and herded together with blows from rifle-butts on Jonas-Daniel-Meyer-plein. The Dutch population, who had solidarity with their Jewish fellow-citizens, were outraged. The Resistance Movement distributed leaflets and called for public protest against these arbitrary measures.

On 25th February the workers, employees and officials of the City of Amsterdam went on strike under the eyes of the German occupying power. Zaandam, Hilversum, Utrecht and Rotterdam followed their example.

The Commander of the *Wehrmacht* in the Netherlands imposed martial law in Amsterdam and declared a state of emergency. All the well-known workers' leaders were arrested, eighteen resistance fighters were shot and many others imprisoned. Four police battalions had to be sent in to crush the strike. The Jewish hostages went to Buchenwald and, from there, on to Mauthausen, where they were all brutally tortured to death.

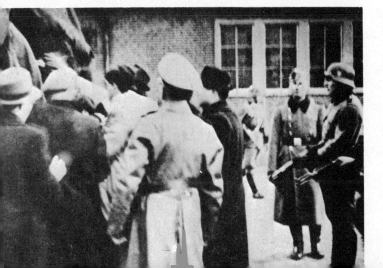

"No Jews allowed", Holland, 1940

1. Jews who have completed their sixth year of age are forbidden to appear in public without a Jewish star.
2. The Jewish star consists of a six-pointed star, the size of the palm of a hand, drawn in black on yellow material, with the inscription "Jew" in black. It is to be worn on the left breast of clothing, clearly visible and strongly sewn on.

Police order on the identification of the Jews in Germany, 1st September 1941

On the Way to the Assembly Point

Registration *(right)*

It is expected that from the middle of July or the beginning of August of this year special trains will run daily with 1000 persons in each. In the first instance, about 40,000 Jews from occupied French territory, 40,000 Jews from the Netherlands and 10,000 Jews from Belgium will be evacuated for labour mobilisation in Auschwitz Camp . . .

I would ask you to take note of the above, and assume that there are no objections to these measures on the part of the Foreign Ministry.

SS-Obersturmbannfuehrer Eichmann, RSHA, to Rademacher, Legation Councillor, Foreign Ministry, 22nd June 1942

114

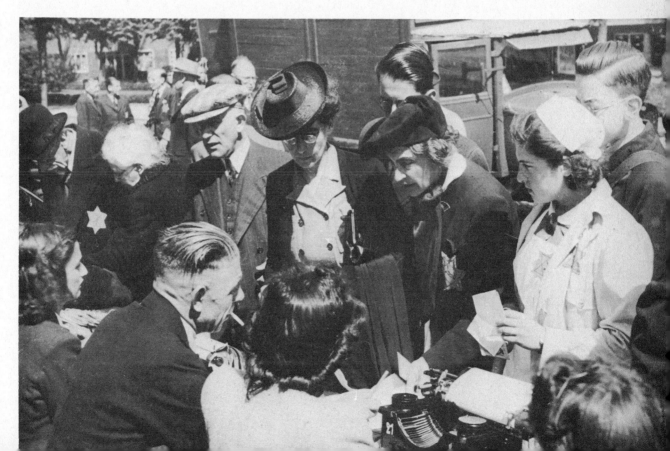

Amsterdam, Summer 1943

Protest against the detestable persecution of Jews!!!
Organise self-defence in the factories and districts!!!
Solidarity with the hard-hit Jewish section of the working people!!!
Snatch the Jewish children from Nazi violence—take them into your family!!!
Strike!!! Strike!!! Strike!!!
Solidarity!!! Courage!!!

Fight proudly for the liberation of our country!!!

Dutch Resistance Movement leaflet

Deportations in Wuerzburg, Germany, and Drancy, France *(right)*

Identity Cards from the Dead of Lodz Ghetto *(pages 120-1)*

SS-Obersturmfuehrer Eichmann by way of introduction first spoke on the further evacuation of 55,000 Jews from Altreich, Ostmark and the Protectorate. Among others, Prague, with 20,000, and Vienna, with 18,000 Jews due for evacuation, are involved in this respect to the greatest extent. Duesseldorf has again been allotted a deportation of 1000 Jews . . .

The Jews are not under any circumstances to come to know of the preparations for the evacuation. Absolute secrecy is therefore essential . . .

There followed an exchange of experiences between the Gestapo stations which had already carried out evacuations and others that were faced with this, for them, new task.

Report of a conference at the RSHA, Dept. IV B 4, 6th March 1942

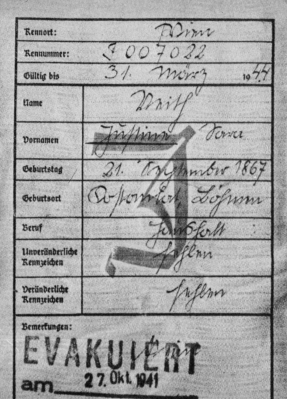

Kennort:	Wien
Kennnummer:	J 007022
Gültig bis	31. März 1944
Name	Weiß
Vornamen	Justine Sara
Geburtstag	21. September 1867
Geburtsort	Osserbet, Böhmen
Beruf	Hausfrau
Unveränderliche Kennzeichen	fehlen
Veränderliche Kennzeichen	fehlen
Bemerkungen:	EVAKUIERT am 27. Okt. 1941

Justine Sara Veitl
(Unterschrift des Kennkarteninhabers)

Wien, den 1. April 1939

Der Polizeipräsident
(Ausstellende Behörde)
i.A.

(Unterschrift des ausfertigenden Beamten)

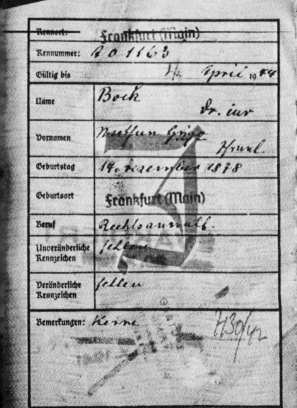

Kennort:	Frankfurt (Main)
Kennnummer:	A 01163
Gültig bis	14. April 1944
Name	Bock dr. iur
Vornamen	Nathan Georg Israel
Geburtstag	14. Dezember 1878
Geburtsort	Frankfurt (Main)
Beruf	Rechtsanwalt
Unveränderliche Kennzeichen	fehlen
Veränderliche Kennzeichen	fehlen
Bemerkungen:	keine

Hugo Israel Bock
(Unterschrift des Kennkarteninhabers)

Frankfurt (Main) den 5. April 1939

Der Polizeipräsident
(Ausstellende Behörde)

(Unterschrift des ausfertigenden Beamten)

Kennort:	Köln - Stadt
Kennnummer:	J 07265
Gültig bis	17. November 19 44
Name	Winter
Vornamen	Leonhard Israel
Geburtstag	21. Dezember 1875
Geburtsort	Roschenbroich b. Gladbach
Beruf	Verwalter
Unveränderliche Kennzeichen	fehlen
Veränderliche Kennzeichen	fehlen
Bemerkungen:	keine

3. —
5790

Rechter Zeigefinger

Linker Zeigefinger

Leonhard Israel Winter
(Unterschrift des Kennkarteninhabers)

Köln, den 18. NOV. 1939 19

Der Polizei-
(Ausstellende Behörde)

Sixewsk
(Unterschrift des ausfertigenden Beamten)

Kennort:	Berlin
Kennnummer:	K 492 982
Gültig bis	5. Februar 19 44
Name	Roser geb. Adam
Vornamen	Martha Sara
Geburtstag	19. Juli 1870
Geburtsort	Gumbinnen
Beruf	ohne
Unveränderliche Kennzeichen	fehlen
Veränderliche Kennzeichen	fehlen
Bemerkungen:	keine

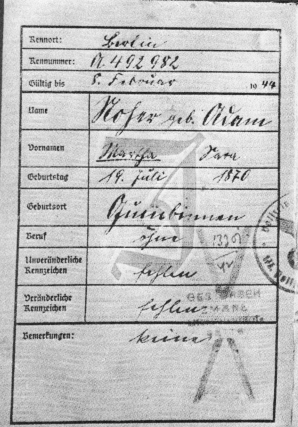

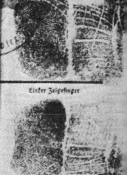

Rechter Zeigefinger

Linker Zeigefinger

Martha Sara Roser
(Unterschrift des Kennkarteninhabers)

Berlin-Schöneberg, den 8. Feb. 1939 19

Der Polizei-Präsident in Berlin
(Ausstellende Behörde)

(Unterschrift des ausfertigenden Beamten)

Shortly afterwards Eichmann came to Auschwitz and disclosed to me the plans for the operations as they affected the various countries concerned. I cannot remember the exact order in which they were to take place. First was to come the eastern part of Upper Silesia and the neighbouring parts of Polish territory under German rule, then, depending on the situation, simultaneously Jews from Germany and Czechoslovakia, and finally the Jews from the West: France, Belgium and Holland. He also told me the approximate number of transports that might be expected, but I can no longer remember these. We discussed the ways and means of effecting the extermination. This could only be done by gassing, since it would have been absolutely impossible to dispose by shooting of the large numbers of people that were expected, and it would have placed too heavy a burden on the SS men who had to carry it out, especially because of the women and children among the victims.

The Commandant of Auschwitz

122

For obvious reasons, Auschwitz Camp has requested once again that Jews to be evacuated in no way receive any disquieting information whatsoever before the evacuation regarding the kind of employment that awaits them. Please note and observe.

I ask in particular that the escort parties should be regularly instructed also during the journey not to let fall any hints whatsoever that would lead to resistance on the part of the Jews, or to make any speculations as to how they will be accommodated, etc. Because of extremely urgent labour projects, Auschwitz must insist on being able to take charge of and distribute the transports as smoothly as possible!

Teleprinter message from the RSHA to the Commanders of the Security Police in the Hague, Paris, Brussels and Metz, 29th April 1943

123

In the meantime, 4000 stateless Jews have already been deported from Drancy to the Auschwitz concentration camp in transport trains with 1000 in each . . .

By the end of July a total of 13,000 Jews have already been evacuated from the occupied territory of France. By the end of August 26,000 Jews will have left French soil.

With the agreement of the *Reichssicherheitshauptamt* the Jewish children are also being deported . . .

The transport plan for the month of August so far likewise envisages 13 trains.

Communication to the General Staff of the Military Commander-in-Chief in France, 30th July 1942

Collection Point in Amsterdam *(right)*

Velodrome d'hiver, Paris, 16th July 1942

Seeking Refuge at the Swiss Legation, Budapest

"Resettlement" in Budapest *(left)*

In some countries the authorities succeeded in avoiding large-scale deportations, as in Denmark and Norway, or at least in delaying them for a long period, as in Hungary and Slovakia. Sweden, Switzerland and some other states issued passports to the persecuted Jews to save them from the grip of the Gestapo.

The Swedish Legation in Budapest alone distributed over 15,000 safe-conducts. After the fascist *coup* in October 1944, when the "Arrow Cross" fascists were carrying out bloody pogroms, Sweden declared many Jewish houses as extra-territorial and saved the lives of the occupants.

Deportation in Bulgaria and Holland (right)

Some of Hitler Germany's allies also opposed the policy of extermination. The victims of persecution found refuge in Italy and the Italian occupied territories of France and Yugoslavia so long as the German *Wehrmacht* had not yet marched in.

Bulgaria extradited only the ''stateless'' Jews from the annexed territories of Macedonia and Thrace. For the majority of Jews in occupied Europe, however, there was no escape.

The German Jews walked the longest *via dolorosa* and passed through all its stations. They died in the ghettos of Lodz and Theresienstadt, in the execution pits of Riga and Minsk—and in the gas chambers of Auschwitz and Treblinka.

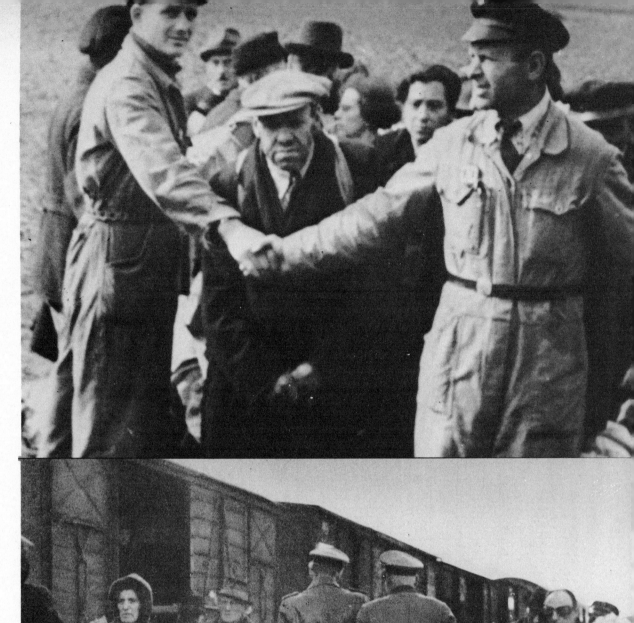

Evacuation to Auschwitz

132

The most important thing to me is, now as ever, that as many Jews as is humanly possible be removed to the East. I wish to be kept constantly informed in the short monthly reports of the Security Police how many Jews have been removed each month and how many are left at that juncture.

Heinrich Himmler, 19th April 1943

The Death Camps

The concentration camps, with their countless subsidiary camps and outdoor working parties, stretched like a giant net over the whole of Germany. They were within easy reach of each of the larger towns. There names penetrated throughout the entire world. Sachsenhausen, Dachau, Buchenwald, Mauthausen, Ravensbrueck taught the peoples of Europe a new German geography. More and more camps were built throughout the occupied territories. There were various categories, various degrees of cruelty, but everywhere the prisoners could expect brutal ill-treatment, starvation, sickness, hard labour and death. People died of exhaustion, were murdered, or threw themselves in despair on to the electrified barbed wire.

The monstrous programme of the ''final solution'' demanded different methods. In Germany mental patients had already been suffocated by gas in air-tight chambers, on the pretext of ''euthanasia''. This technique was now applied on a large scale. The extermination camps came into being on Polish soil: Chelmno, Belsec, Sobibor and Treblinka. Apart from the clearing-up squads, prisoners did not live in these camps. They were killed immediately after their arrival. There were also combined extermination and concentration camps, such as Maidanek and, above all, Auschwitz-Birkenau, the largest forced-labour combine in Hitler's Reich, and, at the same time, the largest human slaughterhouse. Its four crematoria attained a ''daily capacity'' of more than 9000 people gassed and burned. With the advent of the gas chamber, mass murder became an industry. More people went there than could ever have been shot. The death factories swallowed them all. Those who did not suffocate in the gas were worked to death; and those who did not die at once were dead within three months.

Hell on earth awaited those who were picked out at the ''selection'' as being fit for work. Neither photographs nor text can make us realise ourselves what it was like to stand on disciplinary parade for eight hours in the blazing sun or to have one's temperature reduced to 82 degrees in icy water; to be strapped to the whipping block or to witness one's comrades being hanged; to carry heavy cement sacks about, trembling with weakness, or to do knee-bends for the amusement of the guards, knowing all the time that anyone who broke down would be beaten to death.

This was the indirect road to death—life under the constant threat of the smoking chimneys—on short-term hire for the benefit of the contractors. ''Extermination through labour'' was the official name for it. For three *Reichsmarks* a day, the SS hired out the prisoners as cheap labour in the Silesian coalmines and the evacuated armaments factories that had settled like parasites in the neighbourhood of the camp. Their names: Siemens-Schuckert, Krupp and, above all, I.G.-Farben, which even built its own subsidiary camp. Women, as well as men, worked to the point of physical collapse. They were a modern slave army which gave up to the gas chamber every day those who had become ''unfit for service'' and which was replenished again and again by fresh deliveries of prisoners.

Murder thus became a business enterprise. The physical and commercial exploitation of man was perfected into a watertight system. He was robbed of his valuables and his clothes, the members of his family who were unable to work were killed. His labour power was exploited to the point of complete physical exhaustion, or his body was mutilated by medical experiments. Gold teeth were extracted from his corpse and his ashes used as fertiliser. Men were killed individually and by the wagon-load. The murderers kept a book recording their deeds because one wanted to know what one was doing and because one's superiors had to know, and because no-one thought it possible that it would ever come to an end.

The transport trains rolled on, year after year. The Foreign Ministry saw to the necessary diplomatic agreements, the Gestapo organised the capture of men, the Ministry of Transport worked out the time-tables and the camp commandants in Auschwitz built bigger and bigger extermination installations.

We read the accounts of the few who survived this inferno, and the unbelievable notes that the murderers wrote in their files confirming these statements. The more we read, the less we comprehend. Yet none of these reports can adequately convey the reality. Human language has no words for it.

An Eye-witness Reports

The next day we went to Belsec. A small station had been built especially for this purpose on a hill just north of the Lublin-Lemberg Chaussee in the left corner of the demarcation line. South of the road some houses with the notice *"Sonderkommando der Waffen-SS"*. As *Polizeihauptmann* Wirth, the actual head of the whole killing installations, was not yet there, Globocnik introduced me to *SS-Hauptsturmfuehrer* Obermeyer (from Pirmasens). The latter only let me see that afternoon what he had to show me. I did not see any dead that day, but in the hot August weather the whole place smelt like the plague and there were millions of flies everywhere. Right by the small two-track station there was a large shed, the so-called cloakroom, with a large counter where valuables were handed over. Then there was a room containing about 100 chairs—the barber's room. Then an outdoor path under birch-trees, with a double barbed-wire fence on the left and right, with the sign: "To the inhalation and bathrooms". In front of us a sort of bath-house with geraniums, then a few steps, and then three rooms each on the right and left, 5 × 5 m., 1·9 m. high, with wooden doors like garages. In the rear wall, hardly visible in the darkness, large sliding doors. On the roof, as a "witty little joke", the Star of David! In front of the building a notice: Heckenholt Institute. More than that I was not able to see that afternoon.

Shortly before seven the next morning I was informed: "The first transport is coming in ten minutes!" The first train from Lemberg did in fact arrive in a few minutes. Forty-five wagons containing 6700 people, of whom 1450 were already dead on arrival. Children were looking out from behind the barred windows, their faces dreadfully pale and frightened, their eyes filled with the fear of death, besides men and women. The train came into the station: 200 Ukrainians tore open the doors and drove people out of the wagons with their leather whips. A big loudspeaker gave further instructions: undress completely, take off artificial limbs, spectacles, etc. Give up valuables at the counter without credit notes or receipts. Tie shoes together carefully (for textile salvage), otherwise in the pile of shoes, which was a good 25 m. high, no-one could have found a pair that matched. Then the women and children went to the barber who cut off all their hair with two or three chops with the scissors and stuffed it into potato sacks. "That is put to some special use in U-boats—for caulking or something like that," the SS Corporal on duty told me. Then the procession started to move. With a lovely young girl at the front, they all walked along the path, all naked, men, women and children, without their artificial limbs. I stood with *Hauptmann* Wirth up on the ramp between the chambers. Mothers with their babies at the breast came up, hesitated, and entered the death chambers! A sturdy SS man stood in the corner and told the wretched people in a clerical tone of voice: "Nothing at all is going to happen to you! You must take a deep breath in the chambers. That expands the lungs. This inhalation is necessary because of illnesses and infection." When asked what was going to happen to them, he answered: "Well, of course, the men must work, building houses and roads, but the women don't have to work. Only if they want to, they can help with the housework or in the kitchen." This gave some of these poor people a glimmer of hope that lasted long enough for them to take the few steps into the chambers without resisting. The majority realised—the smell told them what their fate was to be! So they climbed the steps and then they saw everything. Mothers with babies at the breast, naked little children, adults, men, women—all naked. They hesitated, but they went into the gas chambers, pushed on by those behind them, or driven in by the leather whips of the SS. Most of them without saying a word. A Jewess of about 40, with eyes blazing, called down upon the heads of the murderers the blood being spilt here. *Hauptmann* Wirth personally gave her five or six lashes in the face with his riding-whip. Then she too disappeared into the chamber. Many people were praying. I prayed with them. I pressed myself into a corner and cried aloud to my God and theirs. How gladly I would have gone with them into the chambers. How gladly I would have died their death with them. Then they would have found a uniformed SS officer in their chambers. The matter would have been treated as a case of death by misadventure and dealt with: missing presumed dead, unheralded and unsung. But I could not do that yet. First I had to make known what I had seen here! The chambers filled. Cram them well in—*Hauptmann* Wirth had ordered. People were standing on each other's feet. 700–800 on 25 square metres, in 45 cubic metres! The SS forced as many in together as was physically possible. The doors closed. Meanwhile the others were waiting outside in the open air, naked ... Now at last I understood why the whole installation was called the Heckenholt Institute. Heckenholt was the driver of the diesel engine—a minor technician who was also the builder of this installation. The people were to be killed with diesel exhaust fumes. But the diesel did not work! *Hauptmann* Wirth came. He was obviously embarrassed that this had to happen on the very day that I was there. Yes, I saw everything! And I waited. My stop-watch had recorded it all well. 50 minutes 70 seconds—the diesel did not start! The people were waiting in the gas chambers. In vain! We heard them weeping, sobbing . . . *Hauptmann* Wirth struck the Ukrainian who was supposed to be helping *Unterscharfuehrer* Heckenholt mend the diesel. The whip hit him in the face 13 or 14 times. After 2 hours 49 minutes—the stop-watch had recorded it all well— the diesel started. Up till then people were alive in these four chambers, four times 750 people in four times 45 cubic metres! Another 25 minutes went by. True, many were now dead. One could see that through the little glass window through which the electric light lit up the chamber for a moment. After 28 minutes only a few were still alive. At last, after 32 minutes everyone was dead! Men of the work squad opened the wooden doors from the other side. They—Jews themselves—had been promised their freedom and a certain percentage of all valuables found in payment for the ghastly duty they performed. The dead were standing upright like basalt pillars, pressed together in the chambers. There would not have been room to fall down or even to bend over. One could tell the families, even in death. They were still holding hands, stiffened in death, so that it was difficult to tear them apart in order to clear the chamber for the next load. The corpses were thrown out—wet with sweat and urine, soiled with excrement, menstrual blood on their legs. Children's bodies flew through the air. There was no time to lose. The whips of the Ukrainians whistled down on the backs of the work squad. Two dozen dentists opened the mouths with hooks and looked for gold. Gold on the right, without gold on the left. Other dentists used pliers and hammers to break gold teeth and crowns out of the jaws. . . . The naked corpses were carried in wooden barrows just a few metres away to pits of 100 by 20 by 12 metres. After some days the putrefying bodies swelled up and then, a short time later, collapsed violently so that a new batch could be thrown on top of them. Then 10 cm. of sand was strewn over it so that only a few single heads and arms stuck out. In one of these spots I saw Jews clambering about on the corpses in the pits and working. I was told that by an oversight those who were already dead when the transport arrived had not been undressed. Because of the textiles and valuables, which they would otherwise have taken with them to the grave, this had of course to be rectified. Nobody took any trouble either in Belsec or in Treblinka to record or count those who were killed. The figures were only estimates based on the capacity of the wagons . . .

The next day—the 19th August 1942—we went in *Hauptmann* Wirth's car to Treblinka, 120 km. NNE of Warsaw. The installation was somewhat similar to that in Belsec except that it was larger. Eight gas chambers and veritable mountains of cases, textiles and underclothes. A banquet in the dining-hall was laid on in our honour in typical Himmlerite Old German style. The meal was simple, but there was masses of everything. Himmler himself had ordered that the men of these *Kommandos* should receive as much meat, butter and other things, particularly alcohol, as they wanted.

We then went by car to Warsaw. After I had tried in vain to find a bed in a sleeper, I met in the train the Secretary of the Swedish Legation in Berlin, Baron von Otter. I told him all this while the shocking experiences were still fresh in my mind, with the request that he inform his government and the Allies at once, as every day's delay would cost further thousands and tens of thousands their lives . . . I then met Mr. von Otter two more times at the Swedish Legation. In the meantime he had reported to Stockholm and informed me this report had had a considerable effect on Swedish-German relations. I tried to give an account of the same matter to the Papal Nuncio in Berlin. There I was asked if I was a soldier. Thereupon further conversation with me was refused and I was requested to leave the Embassy of His Holiness. After leaving the Papal Embassy, I was followed by a policeman on a bicycle. He cycled past me a little way, dismounted and then, in-explicably, let me go. I then informed hundreds of public figures about all this, including the syndic of the Catholic Bishops of Berlin, Dr. Winter, with the express request that he forward the information to the Papal See.

Handwritten account of SS-Obersturmfuehrer Kurt Gerstein, 4th May 1945, in Rottweil

The Commandant of Auschwitz gives Evidence

I, Rudolf Franz Ferdinand Hoess, being first duly sworn, depose and say as follows:

1. I am forty-six years old, and have been a member of the NSDAP since 1922; a member of the SS since 1934; a member of the *Waffen-SS* since 1939. I was a member from 1st December 1934 of the SS Guard Unit, the so-called *Totenkopfverband.*

2. I have been constantly associated with the administration of concentration camps since 1934, serving at Dachau until 1938; then as Adjutant in Sachsenhausen from 1938 to 1st May 1940, when I was appointed Commandant of Auschwitz. I commanded Auschwitz until 1st December 1943, and estimate that at least 2,500,000 victims were executed and exterminated there by gassing and burning, and at least another half-million succumbed to starvation and disease, making a total dead of about 3,000,000. This figure represents about 70 or 80 per cent of all persons sent to Auschwitz as prisoners, the remainder having been selected and used for slave labour in the concentration-camp industries. Included among the executed and burnt were approximately 20,000 Russian prisoners of war . . . The remainder of the total number of victims included about 100,000 German Jews, and great numbers of citizens, mostly Jewish, from Holland, France, Belgium, Poland, Hungary, Czechoslovakia, Greece and other countries. We executed about 400,000 Hungarian Jews alone at Auschwitz in the summer of 1944.

6. The "final solution" of the Jewish question meant the complete extermination of all Jews in Europe. I was ordered to establish extermination facilities at Auschwitz in June 1941. At that time, there were already in the *Generalgouvernement* three other extermination camps: Belsec, Treblinka and Wolzek. These camps were under the *Einsatzkommando* of the Security Police and SD. I visited Treblinka to find out how they carried out their extermination. The Camp Commandant at Treblinka told me that he had liquidated 80,000 in the course of one half-year. He was principally concerned with liquidating all the Jews from the Warsaw Ghetto. He used monoxide gas and I did not think that his methods were very efficient. So when I set up the extermination building at Auschwitz, I used Cyclone B, which was a crystallised prussic acid which we dropped into the death chamber from a small opening. It took from 3 to 15 minutes to kill the people in the death chamber, depending upon climatic conditions. We knew when the people were dead because their screaming stopped. We usually waited about one half-hour before we opened the doors and removed the bodies. After the bodies were removed our *Sonderkommandos* took off their rings and extracted the gold from the teeth of the corpses.

7. Another improvement we made over Treblinka was that we built our gas chambers to accommodate 2000 people at one time, whereas at Treblinka their gas chambers only accommodated 200 people each. The way we selected our victims was as follows: we had two SS doctors on duty at Auschwitz to examine the incoming transports of prisoners. The prisoners would be marched by one of the doctors who would make spot decisions as they walked by. Those who were fit for work were sent into the camp. Others were sent immediately to the extermination plants. Children of tender years were invariably exterminated since by reason of their youth they were unable to work. Still another improvement we made over Treblinka was that at Treblinka the victims almost always knew that they were to be exterminated and at Auschwitz we endeavoured to fool the victims into thinking that they were to go through a delousing process. Of course, frequently they realised our true intentions and we sometimes had riots and difficulties due to that fact. Very frequently women would hide their children under the clothes, but of course when we found them we would send the children in to be exterminated. We were required to carry out these exterminations in secrecy, but of course the foul and nauseating stench from the continuous burning of bodies permeated the entire area and all of the people living in the surrounding communities knew that exterminations were going on at Auschwitz.

Affidavit of SS-Obersturmfuehrer Rudolf Hoess, 5th April 1946, in Nuremberg

An SS Doctor keeps a Diary

31st August 1942

Tropical atmosphere with 38 degrees in the shade, dust and a countless number of flies! Food in the officers' home excellent. This evening we had, e.g., pickled duck's liver for 0.40 Reichsmarks, with stuffed tomatoes, tomato salad, etc. Water is contaminated so we drink soda-water, which is provided free of charge (Mattoni). First inoculation against typhus. Photograph taken for the camp identity card.

2nd September 1942

At 3.0 a.m. attended a *Sonderaktion* for the first time. Compared with this, Dante's Inferno seems almost a comedy. Auschwitz is not called the extermination camp for nothing!

3rd September 1942

Suffering for the first time from one of those attacks of diarrhoea with vomiting and recurring colic-type pains that occur here in the camp. As I have not drunk a drop of water, that cannot be the cause. It cannot be the bread either because those who have eaten only white (dietary) bread also fall sick. Most probably it is due to the unhealthy continental and very dry tropical atmosphere with its large quantities of dust and noxious insects (flies).

5th September 1942

Was at a *Sonderaktion* from FKL (prisoners unfit for work) this afternoon: horror of horrors. *Hauptscharfuehrer* Thilo, medical officer, was right when he told me that here we were at the *anus mundi*. At about 8.0 p.m. was again at a *Sonderaktion* from Holland. The men volunteer for these operations because of the special issue, consisting of a fifth of a litre of *Schnaps*, five cigarettes, 100 g. sausage and bread. On duty today and tomorrow (Sunday).

6th September 1942

Excellent meal today, Sunday: tomato soup, half-chicken with potatoes and red cabbage (20 g. fat), dessert and delicious vanilla ice-cream. After the meal, welcome to the new garrison medical officer, *Obersturmfuehrer* Wirth, who was born in Waldbroel. *Sturmbannfuehrer* Fietsch in Prague was his former regimental officer. I have now been in camp a week, but I have not yet completely got rid of the fleas in my hotel room, in spite of all counter-measures with Flit (Cuprex), etc. . . 8.0 p.m. outside at a *Sonderaktion* again.

Second inoculation against typhus. Rainy and cooler today.   7th September 1942

9th September 1942

This morning I received from Prof. Dr. Hallermann, my lawyer in Muenster, the highly welcome information that I was divorced from my wife on the 1st of this month.

Later, in my capacity as doctor, was present at the punishment by whipping of eight prisoners and an execution by small-bore rifles. Was given soap-flakes and two bars of soap. In the evening at another *Sonderaktion* (fourth time).

In the morning at a *Sonderaktion* (fifth time).   10th September 1942

14th September 1942

Auschwitz sickness for the second time. Temperature 37·8. Today had the third and last injection against typhus.

17th September 1942

Ordered an all-weather coat from the outfitters in Berlin. Tailor's measurements: to waist 48, total length 81, chest 107, waist 100, hips 124. Attached a uniform priority voucher, i.e. for a uniform weather-protection coat. Visited the Birkenau women's camp today with Dr. Meyer.

20th September 1942

This Sunday afternoon from 3—6 o'clock listened to a concert given by the camp orchestra in beautiful sunshine. Conducted by conductor of the Warsaw State Opera. 80 musicians. For dinner there was roast pork. For supper baked tench.

From the diary of SS Hauptsturmfuehrer Prof. Kremer, M.D.

Prisoners give Evidence

Kai Feinberg: The transport from Stettin to Auschwitz lasted three days and three nights. We were transported in cattle wagons, about 45 persons, men, women and children in one closed wagon. For the whole three days and three nights we had nothing to eat and nothing to drink, and we were not allowed to relieve ourselves anywhere other than in the wagon. The wagon was locked.

Marc Klein: When at last our wagon door was opened, SS and prisoners in striped suits drove us out brutally and with blows from sticks, and herded us to the far end of the platform. The men were separated from women and children and heart-rending scenes took place. At lightning speed we passed the inspection of an SS doctor who separated us into two groups by a sign with his stick.

Soon my group consisted of about 200 heads. Mostly young men and those who looked particularly healthy. We had to form fives and then started the march to Auschwitz, four kilometres away . . . It took weeks and months before we slowly realised that the separation on the platform at Birkenau was just the prelude to total extermination, and that with the exception of healthy young women, all the deportees who we had left on the platform had been without exception gassed and burned that very day.

Marie Claude Vaillant-Couturier: We were led into a large barrack and then taken for disinfection. There our heads were shaved and the registration number tattooed on our forearms. After that we were taken into a large room to take a steambath and an ice-cold shower. All this happened in the presence of SS men and women, although we had to undress completely. Then we were given torn and dirty clothing, a woollen skirt and a jacket of similar material.

After that we were taken to the block where we were to live. There were no beds, only bunks measuring two by two metres, and there nine of us had to sleep the first night without any mattress or blanket. We remained in blocks of this kind for several months. We could not sleep all night, because every time one of the nine moved—this happened unceasingly because we were all ill—she disturbed the whole row.

At 3.30 in the morning the shouting of the guards woke us up, and with cudgel blows we were driven from our bunks to go to roll-call. Nothing in the world could release us from going to the roll-call; even those who were dying had to be dragged there. We had to stand there in rows of five until dawn, that is 7 or 8 o'clock in the morning, in winter; and when there was a fog, sometimes until noon. Then the commandos would start on their way to work.

The work at Auschwitz consisted of clearing demolished houses, road building, and especially the draining of marshland . . . During the work the SS men and women who stood guard over us would beat us with cudgels and set their dogs on us. Many of our friends had their legs torn by the dogs.

Noack Treister: A working-party of about 100 men lost about 10 prisoners per day. The prisoners died of malnutrition, as a result of accidents at work, etc. The food was bad and the clothing inadequate . . . There were no washing facilities or soap to keep our clothes clean. The underclothes that I gave out came from those who had been gassed in Birkenau.

Gregoire Afrine: There were often public hangings. I remember an average of two to three hangings per week. The pretexts were flimsy. I remember the case of a young French boy, who was just approaching his seventeenth year. In order to have some sort of celebration, he succeeded in getting hold of a piece of bread and half a tin of jam. He was caught by the SS and hanged. The executions were public and the sentences were read out in German and in the mother-tongue of the condemned man. The gallows were erected on the large entrance square that was used for the roll-call.

Robert Levy: How long could one expect death to be postponed? In Birkenau for a prisoner in a working-party it could be postponed for two to three months. At the end of this period he looked like a skeleton . . . A blow from an SS man's fist or from an overseer's cudgel was enough to finish him off, so that he would inevitably be nabbed at the next "*Selektion*".

Forced Labour for Industry

During a supper that the administration of the concentration camp gave us, we made all the arrangements concerning the participation of the really outstanding concentration-camp organisation for the benefit of the *Buna-Werk*.

Dr. Otto Ambros, member of the Executive Board of IG-Farben, Ludwigshafen, to the Board of Directors, 12th April 1941

At the end of 1941, a proposal was made to the Executive Board of *IG-Farben* by the *IG-Bunawerk Auschwitz* (through Ambros and Buetefisch) that on practical grounds the Monowitz concentration camp should be built on the *IG* Auschwitz site. The estimate for building the Monowitz camp was submitted to the Technical Board, and passed on to the Executive Board, who accepted it. The *IG-Bunawerk Auschwitz* was responsible not only for the accommodation, but also for the feeding and guarding of the concentration-camp prisoners at their place of work.

Karl Krauch, Chairman of the Supervisory Board of IG-Farben, at the IG-Farben trial

We were accommodated at the Monowitz special concentration camp. The conditions were intolerable . . . On our first day of work, Christmas Eve, 24th December 1942, we had to work through without food until 3 o'clock in the morning of 25th December. Our work consisted of unloading wagons of iron bars and sacks of cement and heavy ovens . . .

On 5th January 1943 my father was so weakened that he collapsed before my eyes while having to haul along such a 50-kilo [almost 1 cwt.] sack of cement at a running pace. I wanted to help him but was hit and beaten back by an SS man with a stick . . .

One of my father's brothers injured himself in the arm while at work and was gassed. My father's second brother died from weakness while at work in Buna one or two weeks after the death of my father.

I myself withstood the work until 15th January 1943; then I got pneumonia and worked again from 15th February until the end of February. Then I was declared unfit for work because I could no longer walk, and was due to be gassed. As it happened, no lorry going to the gas chambers came to the *Bunawerk* that day and I was therefore taken back to the Auschwitz concentration camp.

Kai Feinberg, former prisoner, at the Nuremberg Trial

Selections, apart from those in the hospital building of Monowitz, took place every 3–6 weeks in the roll-call yard and at the gates of Monowitz when the prisoners were marching out. The prisoners selected were thrown into open lorries—without shoes or underclothes—(this in winter as well) and driven away. These prisoners frequently struggled against this and shrieked. Such lorries had to drive through part of the grounds of the *IG-Werk* . . .

Leon Staischak, former prisoner, at the Nuremberg Trial

Buna (Monowitz) itself had about 10,000 prisoners. In the orderly-room at Monowitz there was a card-index of all the prisoners who had passed through Monowitz or its subsidiary camps in the period from October 1942 until the liberation of the camp. The card-index of those who had died was a great deal larger than that of the living. I estimate—I repeat that I was in charge of the orderly-room for a long time—that at the end the position in Buna (Monowitz) was approx. 10,000 live prisoners as against approx. 120,000 dead, and in the subsidiary camps taken together approx. 35,000 live prisoners as against 250,000 dead.

Dr. Gustav Herzog, former prisoner, at the Nuremberg Trial

Keeping the Books of Death

Reichssicherheitshauptamt   Dr. Berlin Nue. No. 229793 16.12.1942 2100—Gr.—
Transmission of News

To *Reichsfuehrer SS*
now at Field Headquarters   Urgent—secret—

In the course of the increased delivery of workers to the concentration camps, ordered by 30.1.1943, in the field of the Jewish sector the following can proceed:
    1. Total: 45,000 Jews.
    2. Commencement of transport: 11.1.1943.
    Completion of transport: 31.1.1943. (*Reich* Railways are not in a position to prepare special trains for the evacuation in the period from 15.12.1942 to 10.1.1943 due to increased travel by *Wehrmacht* personnel on leave.)
    3. Analysis: The 45,000 Jews are made up of 30,000 Jews from the Bialystok district—10,000 Jews from the Theresienstadt Ghetto. Of these, 5000 Jews capable of work, who were employed up to now on small jobs required in the ghetto, and 5000 in the main incapable of work, including old Jews of over 60, in order on this occasion to reduce somewhat the present level of 48,000 which is too high to be in the interests of the improvement of the ghetto. I ask for special authorisation for this ... 3000 Jews from the occupied Dutch territories. 2000 Jews from Berlin. 45,000. The figure of 45,000 includes the dependants *incapable of work* (old Jews and children). Application of an appropriate standard in discarding the arriving Jews in Auschwitz will result in at least 10,000 to 15,000 workers.

signed: Mueller, SS-Gruppenfuehrer, on behalf of the Chief of the Security Police

No Room for the Living

The Bermuda Conference opened on Monday, 19th April 1943. That day the *New York Times* editorialised that the conference "is important both as a symbol of future co-operation among the United Nations and as the first attempt at international collaboration to mitigate the appalling horror of Hitler's war of extermination since the outbreak of that war. In both aspects it appears pitifully inadequate ... it would seem that even within the war effort, and perhaps even in aid of it, measures can be devised that go beyond palliatives which appear to be designed to assuage the conscience of the reluctant rescuers rather than aid the victims."

The conference justified the *Times'*s prophecy. Even before it got under way the British delegation informed reporters that there was little possibility of immediate aid for the refugees. The Americans stressed in advance the critical shortage of shipping and reiterated Cordell Hull's theory that refugees should be sheltered near their homelands to simplify their eventual return. The victims, so it seemed, would be eager to return to the scene of the crime.

The London *Observer* commented: "Here are the leisurely beach hotels of the Atlantic luxury island, where well-dressed gentlemen assemble to assure each other in the best Geneva fashion that really nothing much can be done ... The opening speeches of the conference have been widely noticed in this country, and noted with dismay and anger. We have been told that this problem is beyond the resources of Britain and America combined ... If Britain and America cannot help, who can? What is so terrible about these speeches is not only their utter insensitiveness to human suffering. It is the implied readiness of the two greatest powers on earth to humiliate themselves, to declare themselves bankrupt and impotent, in order to evade the slight comfort of charity."

With the exception of a brief press release, no report of the Bermuda Conference was ever published.

                           From the book by Arthur D. Morse

Auschwitz-Birkenau

For years the deportation trains went through this gate from all the towns of Europe. They were all crammed to bursting with people, and they all returned empty . . .

The transports that I saw consisted of Polish Jews. They had received no water for days. When the doors of the goods wagons were opened, we were ordered to drive them out with loud shouts. They were completely exhausted and about a hundred had died during the journey. The survivors had to line up in fives. Our function was to take the corpses, the dying and the baggage out of the wagons. The corpses (and these were considered to be also those who could no longer stand upright) were stacked up into a heap. Pieces of baggage and parcels were collected and piled up. Then the railway wagons had to be thoroughly cleaned so that no trace of their terrible load was visible.

Statement of a prisoner

We travelled in locked wagons, closely packed together and half-suffocated. We all said goodbye to each other, for we knew that the ovens and gas chambers were waiting for us. Although we often talked about it, nobody could really imagine what it would be like. When we arrived in Auschwitz in the evening we were taken to Birkenau. When we were still a long way away we could see the sky glowing red as if there was a fire. None of us could imagine that it could be human beings that were burning like that, although we had already been through a lot. There was no smoke coming from the chimneys, only a rain of sparks. People asked the guards what was burning and they replied that it must be bread being baked. Day and night. But we knew that this could not be the case.

Statement of Giza Landau

The way we selected our victims was as follows: we had two SS doctors on duty at Auschwitz to examine the incoming transports of prisoners. These would be marched by one of the doctors, who would make spot decisions as they walked by. Those who were fit to work were sent into the camp. Others were sent immediately to the extermination plants. Children of tender years were invariably exterminated since by reason of their youth they were unable to work.

Rudolf Hoess, Commandant of Auschwitz

On the Way to the Gas Chamber

"Gentlemen, if a generation should ever follow us that is so spineless and weak-kneed as not to understand our great task, then National Socialism shall indeed have been in vain. I am, on the contrary, of the opinion that bronze tablets should be laid recording that we had the courage to carry out this great and so necessary a work."

Odilo Globocnik, Chief of the SS and Police in Lublin

Selection

By 1942, Canada I could no longer keep up with the sorting. Although new huts and sheds were constantly being added and prisoners were sorting day and night, and although the number of persons employed was constantly stepped up and several trucks (often as many as twenty) were loaded daily with the items sorted out, the pile of unsorted luggage went on mounting up. So in 1942, the construction of Canada II warehouse was begun. Thirty newly built huts were crammed to capacity immediately after completion, while mountains of unsorted effects piled up between them.

Rudolf Hoess

Scarcely fifteen minutes later the chimney began to belch thick clouds of a black, sweetish-smelling smoke which bellied across the camp. A bright, sharp flame shot up, six feet high. Soon the stench of burnt fat and hair grew unbearable. And still the lorries drove past, on the same route. We counted sixty batches that night . . . Soon after the last car had disappeared the first lorries came back laden with the luggage and clothes of the dead, which they took to the depot.

Statement of Ella Lingens-Reiner

Waiting for Death

In the early summer of 1944, when up to six trains were arriving in Auschwitz-Birkenau every day, the condemned people frequently waited a whole day outside the gas chambers before their turn came. The "special detachment", who had to clear out the chambers and take the dead to the crematoria, was increased to 800 men. A further 700 prisoners were employed in sorting the luggage of those who had been gassed.

The enormous installations of the extermination camp were all destroyed by the SS before the end of the war. Only in Maidanek can gas chambers and crematoria still be seen today. Of the others only a few photographs have been preserved.

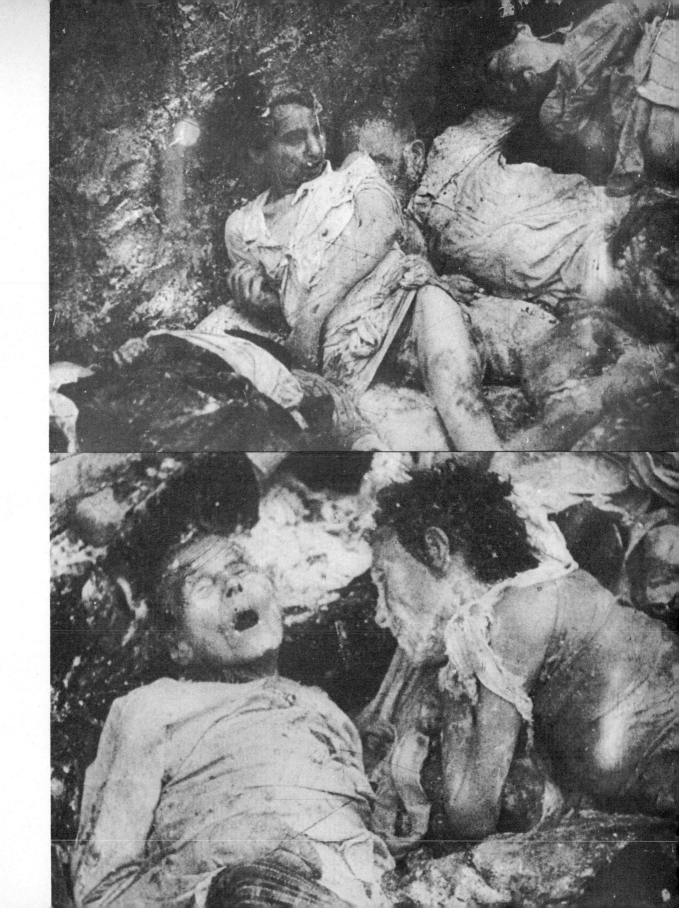

Healthy young people were marched off to the camp for forced labour. Women, as well as men, had to do the heaviest kind of work. They carried heavy loads, built factories and roads, felled trees and drained swamps. They lived in primitive wooden huts under intolerably unhygienic conditions, without sufficient food and without medicines, in constant fear of the SS overseers. With their health ruined by starvation and over-exertion, within the space of a few months they ended up in a hospital barrack or were picked out for the gas chambers at one of the regular "selections". Himmler, master of all the slave camps of the Third *Reich*, was interested in the prisoners only as a source of labour for German industry. When he visited Auschwitz he was shown the manufacturing plant of the combine by Mr. Faust, a representative of IG-Farben (*page 157*)

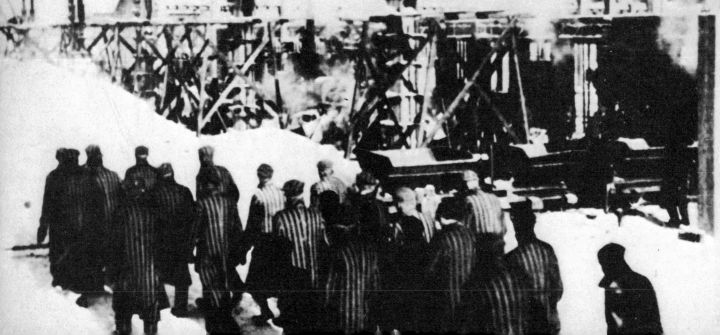

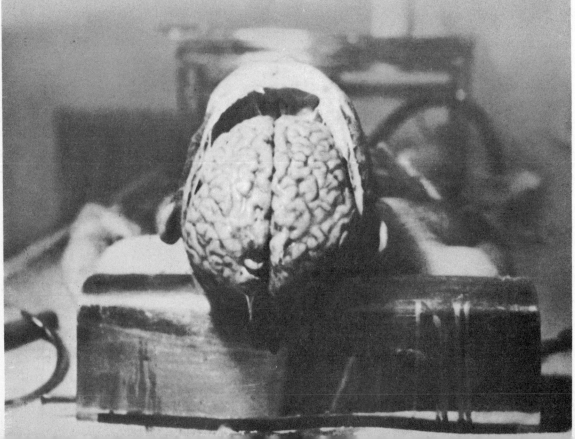

SS doctors misused the prisoners in medical experiments of the utmost cruelty, injecting them with malaria, typhus, gangrene, giving them phosphorous burns, and conducting bone transplants and primitive sterilizations.

In Dachau the human guinea-pigs were locked into low-pressure chambers and subjected to hypothermia in ice-cold water. The dead were then dissected, while the survivors were frequently killed with injections of gasoline. The most common ''experiment'', however, was starvation – until the victims looked like this woman from Budapest.

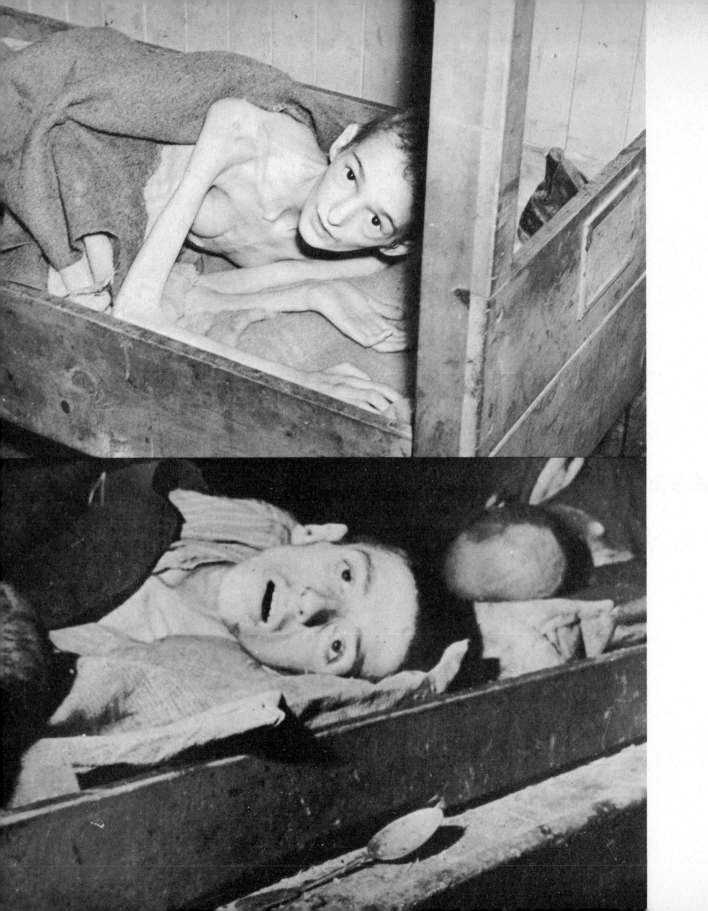

Auschwitz, 12 Nov. 1940
Regarding: Fortnightly report
of field office 1/5
Reference: Order dated 6
Nov. 1940
To the director of *Hauptab-
teilung* 1/5, Department of
Public Works, Berlin-Lichterfelde, Unter den Eichen 126
Nutritional condition of the
prisoners: The food is good
and sufficient. Preparation is
impeccable, clean and appe-
tising.

*SS-Untersturmfuehrer
Schwarz, Auschwitz*

Hitler did not kill the Jews on his own. He had many admirers, many helpers, many patrons. They cannot all be listed. These are four murderers whose names everyone knows: Heydrich, Chief of the Security Police; Eichmann, head of the Gestapo department dealing with Jewish matters; Hoess, Commandant of Auschwitz, and Kramer, his successor.

In the summer of 1944, when even the immense crematoria in Auschwitz became inadequate, the corpses were burned in great open-air pits. Continuously, day and night, people were driven into the gas chambers. These two photographs (left) were taken secretly and smuggled out of the camp by David Szmulewski, a member of the underground resistance organisation.

You will recall the session of the *Reichstag* when I stated: If Jewry imagines for a moment that it can engineer an international world war to annihilate the European races, the result will be not the annihilation of the European races but the annihilation of Jewry in Europe (*applause*).

They always laughed at me for being a prophet. Countless numbers of those who used to laugh then are laughing no longer (*isolated laughs, applause*). Those who are still laughing now, will perhaps not be laughing much longer either (*laughter, loud applause*). This wave will spread out across Europe and across the whole world.

Adolf Hitler on 8th November 1942

Resistance

The passive acceptance by Jewish people of their fate as they went to their death has often been admired. But if anything merits admiration, it is the indomitable will to live of the victims of persecution. In their long heroic struggle, year after year, every day wrested from death, every crust of bread for their children represented a victory over the murderers who had already decreed their death.

Many of those who survived a raid in hiding, or who fled from the ghettos, escaped the firing squads and jumped from the death trains, joined the partisans in the forests.

But even in the ghettos and camps themselves, they took up the struggle. The heroic Warsaw Ghetto Uprising of April 1943 against final extermination is a symbol for all courage and all sacrifice. The SS has left us an illustrated account.

After the large-scale deportations of summer 1942, a precarious calm had fallen on the sparsely populated ghetto. Those remaining behind clung to any hope, however slim. The report that all those who had been deported—a whole town of people—had been killed seemed to them too insane to be believed. It was a long time before they finally grasped what was in store for them all, without exception.

In January 1943, when the deportations were resumed, the first armed outbreak took place. Himmler ordered the destruction of the ghetto. The Jewish Resistance Organisation called upon the condemned to fight. Secretly, during the night, deep trenches were dug in the ground. Primitive underground bunkers were feverishly constructed to serve as protection for the women and children against the manhunters.

On 19th April, the SS stormtroopers broke into the ghetto. They encountered bitter resistance. The youth of the ghetto heroically defended the lives of their mothers, brothers and sisters. Almost without weapons, with despair lending them strength, they fought the SS for every street, every house, every cellar. The fighting lasted for 28 days and nights. For most of them it ended in death.

All those who did not fall in the fighting were transported to the gas chambers in Treblinka. Few only escaped the burning cauldron. But the uprising demonstrated to oppressors and oppressed alike that human self-respect and dignity could not completely be extinguished even in the midst of brutality and murder. In the ghettos of Bialystok and Czenstochowa, the example of Warsaw was followed. Even in the death camps of Treblinka and Sobibor there were bloody uprisings; in Auschwitz-Birkenau courageous prisoners set fire to a crematorium.

The Jews were not alone in this struggle. In France, young people wore the yellow star as a gesture of solidarity. In Holland, workers went on strike in protest against the deportations. In every country, including Germany, there were courageous individuals, priests and workers, officials and officers, who stood up for the victims of persecution, or took them into their homes, thus endangering the lives of their own families.

There were heroes, like Sergeant Anton Schmid, who saved thousands of Jews in Wilna from the firing squad, the manufacturer Oskar Schindler in Crackow, who led his Jewish prisoner-workers to safety towards the end of the war, or that Communist prisoner in Auschwitz, who hid a group of 158 Jewish children in the block for which he was responsible. In Berlin there were brave women who demonstrated publicly for the release of their Jewish husbands, and Provost Lichtenberg who prayed in his church "for the Jews and the wretched prisoners in the concentration camps".

And there was the anonymous army of the European Resistance who, in every country, waged that desperate, silent war against the gas chamber system—a war in which there were no medals to be won, only the guillotine, the gallows or the concentration camp.

Everywhere where there was persecution, resistance emerged. It was not strong enough to halt the mass murder but it could impede it. It breached the ranks of the murderers and snatched single victims from them. Above all, this resistance imparted a moral strength, demonstrating as it did that the power of the enemy was not boundless and that it would eventually come to an end.

The Uprising and Destruction of the Warsaw Ghetto

Extracts from the daily reports of SS-General Stroop

19th April 1943. Ghetto sealed off from 3.00 hours. At 6.00 hours deployment of the *Waffen-SS* in strength of 16/850 for the combing of the remainder of the ghetto. Immediately upon entry strong concerted fire by the Jews and bandits . . .

We succeeded in forcing the enemy to withdraw from the roof-tops and strong-points situated in high positions to the cellars or bunkers and sewers. About 200 Jews were caught in the combing operation. Shock patrols were then deployed against known bunkers with the task of clearing out the occupants and destroying the bunkers. Resultant catch of Jews about 380. The presence of Jews in the sewers was established. Total flooding was carried out, rendering presence impossible.

20th April 1943. The pockets of resistance located in the uninhabited, not yet opened up part of the ghetto were put out of action by an assault squad of the *Wehrmacht*—sappers and flame-throwers . . . The 10-cm. howitzer had dislodged the bands from their fortifications and, as far as can be ascertained, also caused them some casualties. Due to the onset of darkness this *Aktion* had to be broken off.

21st April 1943. Setting fire to the buildings had the result that Jews who were, despite all searching operations, concealed under the roofs or in the cellars and other hiding places, appeared during the night on the outside fronts of the blocks of buildings somehow to escape the fire. Large numbers of Jews—entire families—already on fire, jumped from the windows or tried to let themselves down by means of sheets, etc., tied together. We made sure that these, as well as the other Jews, were liquidated immediately.

22nd April 1943. It is unfortunately impossible to prevent a proportion of the bandits and Jews from hiding in the sewers under the ghetto where they have evaded capture by preventing the flooding. The city administration is not in a position to remove this inconvenience. Smoke-bombs and mixing creosote with the water have also failed to achieve the desired result. Liaison with the *Wehrmacht* excellent.

23rd April 1943. The whole *Aktion* is made more difficult by the cunning tricks employed by the Jews and bandits, e.g. it was discovered that live Jews were being taken to the Jewish cemetery in the corpse carts that collect the dead bodies lying around, and were thus escaping from the ghetto. Permanent guard on the corpse carts had blocked this escape route . . .

Today 3500 Jews from the factories were caught for evacuation. So far a total of 19,450 Jews have been caught for evacuation or have already been transported. Out of these Jews there are at the moment still about 2500 to be loaded. The next train leaves on 24.4.43.

24th April 1943. At 18.15 hours the search party entered the buildings after they had been cordonned off and established the presence of a large number of Jews. As most of these Jews resisted I gave the order to burn them out. Not until the whole street and all the court-yards on both sides were in flames did the Jews, some of them on fire, come out from the blocks of buildings or try to save themselves by jumping from the windows and balconies into the street on to which they had thrown beds, blankets and other things. Time and time again it could be observed that Jews and bandits preferred to return into the flames rather than fall into our hands.

25th April 1943. If last night the sky above the former ghetto was filled with the glow from the fire, this evening an immense sea of fire is to be seen. As with the methodical and regular combing operations a large number of Jews continue to be ferreted out, the *Aktion* will be resumed on 26.4.43. Start 10.00 hours.

Today a total of 27,464 Jews of the former Jewish ghetto of Warsaw were caught.

26th April 1943. It is becoming increasingly obvious that it is now the turn of the toughest and most resistant Jews and bandits. Several times bunkers have been forcibly opened, the occupants of which had not come up to the surface since the beginning of the *Aktion*. In a number of cases the occupants of the bunker were no longer in a position, after the explosion, to crawl up to the surface. According to statements made by Jews caught, a considerable number of the occupants have been driven mad by the heat and smoke and explosions . . .

30 Jews evacuated, 1330 Jews brought up out of bunkers and immediately destroyed. 363 Jews shot in the fighting. Total caught today: 1722 Jews. Total number of Jews caught thus increased to 29,186. In addition, countless Jews have probably perished in the 13 bunkers blown up and in the fires.

27th April 1943. It has been established by the SS men who descended the sewers that the bodies of a great many dead Jews are being washed away by the water.

28th April 1943. Today's results: 1655 Jews caught for evacuation, of which 110 shot in the fighting.

In addition, many Jews were burned in the fire and an unascertainable number destroyed when individual bunkers were blown up.

Today's results bring the total number of caught or destroyed Jews to 33,401. This figure does not include Jews burned or destroyed in bunkers.

29th April 1943. Several sewer shafts have been blown up. Two outlets located outside the ghetto have likewise been made unusable by blowing up or walling up.

Statements by various occupants of bunkers confirm that these Jews have not been outside for 10 days and that as a result of the long duration of this *Grossaktion* their food supplies, etc., are giving out.

30th April 1943. Today a total of 1599 Jews were caught, 179 of which shot in the fighting. This brings the total number of Jews caught so far to 37,359. 3855 Jews were loaded on to the train today. The number of armed Jews caught in the last few days has increased quite a lot.

1st May 1943. A considerable number of the Jews caught were brought up out of the sewers. The systematic blowing up or blocking up of the sewers was continued . . .

A shock patrol has established an unascertainable number of corpses floating in a main sewer under the ghetto.

2nd May 1943. Combing of the whole district of the former ghetto by nine shock patrols, also deployment of a large detachment for cleaning or destruction of a block of buildings situated round the Transavia and Wiszniewski armaments factories . . .

When the above block of buildings was destroyed 120 Jews were caught and countless Jews destroyed when as a result of the fire they jumped down to the inner court-yards from the attics.

In addition many Jews have perished in the flames and a further number have been destroyed by the blowing up of bunkers and sewer outlets.

3rd May 1943. In most cases the Jews use weapons in resisting leaving the bunkers. There are therefore two wounded to report. Some of the Jews and bandits fire pistols with both hands.

4th May 1943. Countless Jews who appeared on the roof-tops during the fire have perished in the flames. Others did not make an appearance on the top storeys until the last minute and could only save themselves from being burned to death by jumping down. Today a total of 2283 Jews have been caught, 204 of which shot, countless Jews destroyed in bunkers and in the fire. The total number of the Jews caught so far has increased to 44,089.

167

5th May 1943. Today also the Jews in various places have put up a resistance before being caught. In several cases the openings/hatches of the bunkers were closed or barred by force from the inside so that a large explosion was the only way to force an opening and destroy the occupants.

6th May 1943. Today particularly those blocks of buildings that were destroyed by fire on May 4th were combed. Although it was hardly to be expected that people would be found alive in them, a whole number of bunkers, which were red-hot inside, were discovered. A total of 1553 Jews discovered in these bunkers and others of the ghetto were caught. 356 Jews were shot when resisting and in the fighting that developed.

7th May 1943. The Jews state that they come out into the fresh air at night as it is becoming intolerable to stay in the bunkers without a break for the long duration of the *Aktion*. An average of 30 to 50 Jews are shot by the shock patrols every night.

From these statements it must be assumed that a considerable number of Jews are still underground in the ghetto.

8th May 1943. According to statements made, there must still be about 3000–4000 Jews in the underground cavities, sewers and bunkers. The undersigned is determined not to terminate this *Grossaktion* until the very last Jew is destroyed.

9th May 1943. The *Grossaktion* carried out today had the following results: 42 bunkers were located by the shock patrols engaged in combing operations. 1037 Jews and bandits were brought up out of these bunkers alive. 319 bandits and Jews were killed in the fighting, apart from the count-less Jews destroyed once again by blowing up the bunkers.

10th May 1943. The resistance put up by the Jews today was unabated. In contrast to previous days, the members of the Jewish main fighter groups still in existence and not destroyed have apparently retreated to the highest ruins accessible to them in order to inflict casualties on the raiding parties by firing on them.

11th May 1943. A total of 931 Jews and bandits were caught. 53 bandits were shot. More lost their lives in bunkers that were blown up and houses that were destroyed. The total number of Jews caught so far has increased to 53,667.

12th May 1943. A considerable number of Jews have probably perished in the flames. As the fire had not burnt itself out by the onset of darkness, the exact number could not be ascertained.

13th May 1943. For two days the few Jews and criminals still in the ghetto have been making use of the hiding-places still provided by the ruins to return at night to the bunkers known to them, eating there and supplying themselves with food for the next day.

14th May 1943. Repeated firing took place on the outer barricade from the Aryan side. The cordon of sentries answered the fire relentlessly.

15th May 1943. The last undamaged block of buildings still in existence in the ghetto was searched through once more and then destroyed by a special raiding-party. In the evening the chapel, mortuary and all the adjoining buildings in the Jewish cemetery were blown up or destroyed by fire.

16th May 1943. The former Jewish quarter of Warsaw is no longer in existence. With the blowing up of the Warsaw Synagogue, the *Grossaktion* was terminated at 20.15 hours . . .

Total number of Jews caught or verifiably exterminated: 56,065.

The Evacuation begins

A few hours ago armed SS detachments with tanks and artillery began the murder of the remaining inhabitants of the ghetto. The ghetto is offering bitter and heroic resistance. The Jewish Fighter Organisation is leading the defence and has collected around itself nearly all the fighter groups. There is an incessant thunder of cannon and great explosions from the ghetto. The whole quarter is bathed in the glow of enormous conflagrations. Aircraft circle above the area of the slaughter. The outcome of this struggle is, of course, a foregone conclusion.

Radio message from the ZOB (Jewish Fighter Organisation) to London, 19th April 1943

Arrest of the Management of the Brauer Factory

Girls, Fighters for the Children's lives *(right)*

The resistance offered by the Jews and bandits could be broken only by energetic and tireless round-the-clock action by the shock patrols. On 23.4.1943 the order came from the *Reichsfuehrer-SS* through the *Hoehere SS- and Polizeifuehrer Ost* in Crackow that the combing of the Warsaw Ghetto be carried out with the utmost severity and relentless tenacity. I decided at this stage, therefore, to undertake the total destruction of the Jewish residential district by burning down whole blocks of buildings, including the blocks next to the armaments factories. One factory after another was systematically evacuated and destroyed by fire.

Stroop Report

Search

The longer the resistance lasted, the tougher became the men of the *Waffen-SS*, the police and the *Wehrmacht*, who set about the performance of their duties in true brotherhood-in-arms and always stood their ground in exemplary and ideal fashion. The engagement frequently lasted from early morning until late into the night.

174

Stroop Report

The March to the "*Umschlagplatz*"

The fire raged . . . with unbelievable intensity. The streets of the ghetto were filled with dense, acrid smoke. It was plain that the Germans were now employing the monstrous tactic of smoking out the ghetto. When they saw they could not break the resistance of the Jewish fighters with weapons, they decided to destroy them by fire. In the buildings thousands of women and children were burned alive. Terrible screams and cries for help could be heard coming from the burning houses. People who had been caught by the flames appeared like living torches at the windows of many buildings.

175

Report of the ZOB, No. 5

Not infrequently, the Jews stayed in the burning buildings until, due to the heat and the fear of being burned alive, they preferred to jump down from the upper storeys, having first thrown down mattresses and other upholstery on the street. With their bones broken, they still tried to crawl across the street to blocks of buildings that were not yet, or only partially, on fire.

Stroop Report

SS-General Juergen Stroop, *"Fuehrer der Grossaktion"*

Brought up from the Bunkers

Beneath the smouldering ruins, far from the spring day, hundreds of us lay on the floor of a bunker, five metres down in complete darkness. Not a ray of daylight could penetrate down here. We only knew by the clock that outside the sun was setting . . . Every night Jews who had left the dark, stuffy dug-outs roamed the streets in search of their families and friends. Every night we saw how rapidly our number was diminishing. The ghetto was rapidly dwindling. Starvation and the discovery of one bunker after the other by German patrols took their toll . . .

Report of Cywia Lubetkin

Life belongs to us too! We too have a right to it! We only have to know how to fight for it! It is easy enough to live if they give you life as a *gracious gift*! It is not so easy when they want to snatch life away from you!

Rise up, people, and fight for your lives!

Every mother shall become a lioness defending her young! No longer shall a father quietly look upon the death of his children! The shame of the first act in our destruction shall not be repeated! May every house become a fortress! Rise up, people, and fight!!! Your salvation lies in fighting! He who fights for his life has the chance of saving himself! We rise up in the name of the fight for the lives of the helpless whom we wish to save and whom we must rouse to action!

From an underground leaflet

The Defenders of the Ghetto are led to their Execution

It is already the eighth day of our life and death struggle . . . The number of victims, the victims of the executions and the fires in which men, women and children perished, is enormous. Our last days are approaching. As long as we can hold a gun in our hands, however, we will resist and fight.

We reject the German ultimatum to surrender. As we see our last days approaching, we call upon you. Do not forget! The day will come when our innocently spilt blood will be avenged. Come to the aid of those escaping from the enemy at the last minute so that they can continue the fight.

Report of the ZOB, 26th April 1943

Executed Ghetto Fighters

In another corner lay a year-old baby. It was not crying or moaning. It probably no longer had the strength. Its little arms and legs were burned. I shall never forget the look of intense pain reflected in its little face . . . The mother's face and arms were completely burned. She could not hold the baby in her arms.

182

Report of P. Elster

The Last Ones are marched away

Our watchword was: Live and die with dignity!

In ghettos and camps we strove to live up to this watchword . . . Despite the greatest terror, extreme hunger and most bitter privation, we upheld it until the martyr's death of Polish Jewry.

183

Report of the Jewish Resistance Movement

Es gibt keinen jüdischen Wohnbezirk —in Warschau mehr!

Liberation

In July 1944 the Soviet Army liberated the Maidanek concentration camp. At the same time nearly half a million Hungarian Jews were still being deported to Auschwitz-Birkenau. For six weeks the ovens burned day and night. Not until the end of November did the SS blow up the crematoria, destroy the camp records and set fire to the huge storehouses containing the belongings of those who had been gassed.

The end of the war dictated the last bloody chapter. Many people in Germany feared the end and tried desperately to flee before the advancing front. Those who were longing for the collapse of the Hitler regime, however, and who were looking forward to their hour of liberation, were transported to the interior on the orders of Himmler. No prisoner was to fall into the hands of the Allies alive. Were the murderers afraid of what the prisoners would have to tell? Did they grudge the return to life of those who had been flayed in mind and body? Or could the torturers not bear the thought that some of their victims might outlive them?

The Allied troops were advancing on Germany from all sides. A race against death began. The camps in the East were evacuated. The prisoners were driven in open lorries, without blankets or coats, through the icy February. There were opportunities to escape, but none of these starving and exhausted people had the strength to crawl away.

In the last weeks of the war the ghoulish trains crossed the railway network of the crumbling *Reich* from one camp to another: stood, were diverted, stopped and went on again. From Auschwitz to Buchenwald, from Buchenwald to Dachau, from Dachau to Belsen. Aimless and unscheduled, they had but one object—to deny their freight its last chance of survival. Frequently, by the time the journey ended near a camp, after many days on a siding, and the wooden doors were finally slid open, the wagon had long since become a mortuary.

The fronts were approaching each other with increasing speed. Many concentration camps had to be evacuated in a great hurry by the SS. Prisoners who were not capable of marching were shot or burned alive in the last few hours. Under the eyes of a shocked German population, the guards drove an army of wretched figures on forced marches along the highways of Thueringen and Mecklenburg to Schleswig-Holstein. If a prisoner collapsed and remained lying by the wayside, he was finished off with a bullet. Bergen-Belsen, which took in the last transports, was an overcrowded mass grave, a death zone where hunger and typhus raged.

The Allied soldiers who liberated the concentration camps were stunned. They saw the gallows and the whipping-block, the crematoria and the storehouses of shoes, clothes, spectacles and human hair. They saw the cases full of gold teeth and wedding rings. They saw the book, kept by the book-keeper of the dead, and they saw the human beings—the dead and the dying. When the first photographs and press reports of the indescribable conditions were published abroad, the civilised world reacted with an outcry of horror and outrage.

The end came too late for many of the few who had managed to survive until then. They no longer had the strength to begin again. For weeks after the liberation, thousands of prisoners were still dying. They were beyond any help. Not until many days later did the Allied doctors make the terrible discovery that many had died whose lives could still perhaps have been saved. They had been too weak to call out or to lift an arm and so had been left to lie unnoticed under the corpses.

Thus ended Hitler's Third *Reich*.

The victory of the Allies prevented the Nazis from completing their extermination programme. The balance-sheet is terrible enough. All calculations, made by comparing population figures, the official records that were uncovered and the investigations in the death camps, came to the unanimous conclusion that about six million Jews had been murdered. Well over a million perished from starvation and disease, almost as many were killed by the guns of the firing squads: all the others went to the gas chambers.

The Last Days

Mauthausen. Obergruppenfuehrer Pohl sent me one day without previous notification 6000 women and children, who had been on the transport for ten days without food. In the icy winter of December 1944 they were transported in open coal-trucks without blankets. On orders of Berlin, I had to start them off on a march to Bergen-Belsen and I assume that they all died . . .

Transports of Jews: In the presence of *Gauleiter* Rainer, Dr. Ueberreiter, Dr. Jury, Baldur von Schirach and others I received the following orders from Himmler: The Jews engaged in the construction of defences "*Suedosten*" must be moved away from all places on foot. Destination: Mauthausen. 60,000 Jews were subsequently to come to Mauthausen. A small fraction of them did in fact arrive. As an example, I mention a transport that set off with 4500 Jews and arrived in Mauthausen with 180 persons. Where the transport which I gave as an example set off from, I do now know. Women and children were without shoes, in rags and covered in lice. There were whole families in the transport, countless numbers of whom had been shot on the way because of general weakness.

Statement of Franz Ziereis, Commandant of Mauthausen

Bergen-Belsen. When they were beaten, they would sometimes suddenly move forward like a herd of cattle, jostling against one another. It was impossible to elicit their names from them. The kindest word did not have the power to move them to talk. A long, fixed, expressionless stare was all. If they made an attempt to reply, their tongues could not reach their palates to produce a sound. One was aware only of their foul breath, which seemed to come up from intestines that were already in a state of decay. That is what the transports in the winter of 1944/45 were like, that winter when death claimed the colossal number of 13,000 internees in the last three months before our liberation.

Statement of Dr. Georg Straka

Oederan. Great excitement already reigned in the camp because at 3 p.m. we had to fall in for departure. The order said: Prisoners and all the overseer personnel fall in for evacuation before the enemy. Destination unknown. At about 8 a.m. we could already hear the rumbling of guns and our hearts beat faster in the hope that it would not come to it after all. When we fell in at 3 p.m., the windows were rattling and the ground shook beneath our feet. Hand in hand with my friend, equipped with a bucket stuffed full with my belongings, we stood, 500 women, in the yard of our camp, to bend once more under the cruel yoke. And this in the face of the Allies, whose voices we could hear and who could not hear our fervent prayers. Under an escort of armed Reserves and Hitler Youth, we left, wrapped in our grey blankets. We walked to the station and were loaded into open cattle trucks.

Statement of Grete Salus

Dachau. 8000 people, Russians, Jews, Germans, including 100 priests, now marched silently through the night, guarded by almost 1000 SS men and many bloodhounds . . . After the first hour I already saw the first bundles lying on the right and left of the road. The two woollen blankets which everybody had to take with them were already too heavy for these emaciated bodies. Soon, however, the first prisoners were already lying at the edge of the road, totally exhausted. We heard shots ring out in the still of the night. The fate of the Auschwitz prisoners seemed to be repeating itself. Do not break down now, at the eleventh hour! We marched 40 km. that night. Before noon we reached the first resting-place, the Muehetal on Lake Starnberg. I fell exhausted on to the forest floor and went to sleep. I was wakened by shots and the shout of "Dog-leader! Dog-leader!" So someone has run away. Let us hope they do not catch him. I heard later that it was a young chaplain from the diocese of Muenster, the first among us who succeeded in escaping . . .

Report of Father Pereira S.J., Treves

The End

Bergen-Belsen. Four days after the American occupation of Buchenwald, British troops of General Dempsey's XI Armoured Division reached the prison camp of Belsen (situated between Hanover and Bremen). Here they found 28,000 women, 11,000 men and 500 children. In Belsen there was not only starvation, but also typhus.

Huge ovens had been built for incinerating the corpses, but in Belsen, as in Buchenwald, the mortality rate was too high for the furnaces to keep pace with the number who were dying daily. Apart from this, here too coal was in increasingly short supply. Reports submitted to the British General, Army Medical Corps, show that in the last few months 30,000 people have died in Belsen. When the British entered there was still—beside great pits filled with the charred remains of bones—a whole number of heaps of corpses. Every pile contained several hundred naked bodies, already in an advanced state of decomposition. General Dempsey's soldiers used excavators to dig out long graves in which 500 or 1000 corpses could be buried at a time. Then the former guards—men and women—had to carry up the bodies of those who had fallen victim to the epidemic diseases or had been starved, suffocated or shot.

It was a week before the heaps of bodies stopped growing and people could at last be interred in the mass graves as soon as they died.

"KZ", illustrated report of the US Information Service in Germany

Buchenwald. The size of the camp is indicated by the fact that its maximum capacity was said to have been 120,000. On 1st April last the number in camp was 80,813. A few days before the arrival of the American forces (11th April), the Nazis removed a large number of prisoners, variously estimated at from 18,000 to 22,000. Some of those whom they wished to remove (because "they knew too much") were able to hide from them. It was impossible to form any accurate estimate of the percentages of various nationalities still remaining in the camp; we met many Jews and non-Jewish Germans, Poles, Hungarians, Czechs, French, Belgians, Russians and others. A detailed report presented to us by representatives of an anti-Fascist committee stated that, up to 1st April, the total number of those who had died or been killed at Buchenwald, or immediately on removal therefrom to subsidiary "extermination camps", was 51,572—at least 17,000 of them since 1st January 1945 . . .

Although the work of cleaning the camp had gone on busily for over a week before our visit, and conditions must therefore have been improved considerably, our immediate and continuing impression was of intense general squalor; the odour of dissolution and disease still pervaded the entire place. One of the first of a number of huts that we entered was one of the best . . .

This hut was one of those now used as transit hospitals for some of the worst cases of malnutrition. Many were unable to speak: they lay in a semi-coma, or following us with their eyes. Others spoke freely, displaying sores and severe scars and bruises which could only have been caused by kicks and blows. They lay on the floor, on and under quilts. All of them were in a state of extreme emaciation. We were told by the US authorities that, since their arrival, the number of deaths had been reduced from about 100 per day to 35 on the day before our visit. The usual clothing was a ragged shirt, vest or cotton jacket, beneath which protruded thighs no thicker than normal wrists. One half-naked skeleton, tottering painfully along the passage as though on stilts, drew himself up when he saw our party, smiled and saluted. The medical members of our Delegation expressed the opinion that a percentage of them could not be expected to survive, even with the treatment they were now receiving, and that a larger percentage, though they might survive, would probably suffer sickness and disablement for the rest of their lives.

Report of a British Parliamentary Delegation

The Balance Sheet

I, Wilhelm Hoettl, hereby declare under oath:
At the end of August 1944 I conversed with *SS-Obersturmbannfuehrer* Adolf Eichmann, whom I had known since 1938. The conversation took place in my apartment in Budapest.

At this time Eichmann was to my knowledge departmental head of Amt IV (Gestapo) of the *Reichssicherheitshauptamt* and was, over and above this, charged by Himmler to get hold of the Jews in all European countries and transport them to Germany. Eichmann was at the time much affected by Rumania's withdrawal from the war which took place in those days. That is why he had visited me to obtain information about the military situation which I received daily from the Hungarian *Honved* (War) Ministry and the Commander of the *Waffen-SS* in Hungary.

He expressed his conviction that Germany had now lost the war and that he personally no longer had a chance. He said that he knew that he would be regarded as a major war criminal by the United Nations because he had millions of Jewish lives on his conscience. I asked him how many it was, to which he replied that the number was in fact a great *Reich* secret but that he would tell me as I would be interested in it as a historian too and as he would probably not return from his command in Rumania. A short time before he had made a report for Himmler, who had wanted to know the exact number of Jews killed. On the basis of his information he had come to the following conclusion:

About four million Jews had been killed in the various extermination camps, while a further 2 million met their death in other ways, the majority being executed by the *Einsatzkommandos* of the Security Police during the campaign against Russia.

He said that Himmler had not been satisfied with the report as in his opinion the number of Jews killed must have been greater than 6 million. Himmler had said that he wished to send a man from his statistics department to Eichmann in order to write a fresh report, on the basis of Eichmann's material, in which the exact figure should be worked out.

I must assume that the information that Eichmann gave me was correct, as of all the people concerned he certainly had the best over-all view of the number of Jews murdered. Firstly, he so to speak "delivered" the Jews to the extermination installations by his *Sonderkommandos* and therefore knew the exact number, and secondly, as Head of Department of Amt IV of the RSHA, which was also responsible for Jewish matters, he certainly knew best the number of Jews who had perished in other ways.

In addition to this, due to the events, Eichmann was certainly in no frame of mind to have any intention of telling me anything that was untrue.

I myself am quite sure of the details of this talk because it had understandably moved me very much and because I had, before the German collapse, already made detailed statements on this matter to an American authority in a neutral country with which I was at that time in contact.

I swear that I have made the above statements voluntarily and without duress and that the above statements are true to the best of my knowledge and belief.

Affidavit of former SS-Sturmbannfuehrer Dr. Wilhelm Hoettl

Lt.-Col. Brookhart: When did you last see Eichmann?
Wisliceny: I last saw Eichmann towards the end of February 1945 in Berlin. At that time he said that if the war were lost he would commit suicide.
Lt.-Col. Brookhart: Did he say anything at that time as to the number of Jews that had been killed?
Wisliceny: Yes, he expressed this in a particularly cynical manner. He said he would leap laughing into the grave because the feeling that he had 5 million people on his conscience would be for him a source of extraordinary satisfaction.

Sworn statement of former SS-Hauptsturmfuehrer Dieter Wisliceny
at Nuremberg, 3rd January 1946

While the war was still going on, the exhumation of the victims began in the liberated territories.

Some months later, the Allied forces advancing through Poland and Germany came upon the great concentration camps, in which a host of human creatures, deformed by disease and privation, were awaiting their liberation. The Allied doctors were often too late. Many prisoners died in the last few days before liberation: many died in the weeks following.

Exhumation in Hungary

Dachau Concentration Camp

To the Camp Commandants of Dachau and Flossenbuerg.
Surrender is out of the question. The camp is to be evacuated immediately. No prisoner must fall into the hands of the enemy alive.

Heinrich Himmler, 4th April 1945

As you view the history of our time, turn and look at the piles of bodies, pause for a short moment and imagine that this poor residue of flesh and bones is *your* father, *your* child, *your* wife, is the one you love. See yourself and those nearest to you, to whom you are devoted heart and soul, thrown naked into the dirt, tortured, starving, killed.

Eugen Kogon

Tens of thousands of children were gassed in Auschwitz. Only 60 pairs of twins, who had been selected by the SS doctors for medical experiments, lived to be liberated by the Red Army. The children willingly showed the photographers the numbers tattooed on their arms.

At this time, there were only 5000 prisoners left in the camp. They had been left behind during the evacuation as being sick and unfit to march. All the others, about 66,000 people, were driven west by the SS on a forced march, during which many of them died.

Auschwitz, 26th January 1945 *(right)*

Blown-up Underground Gas Chamber

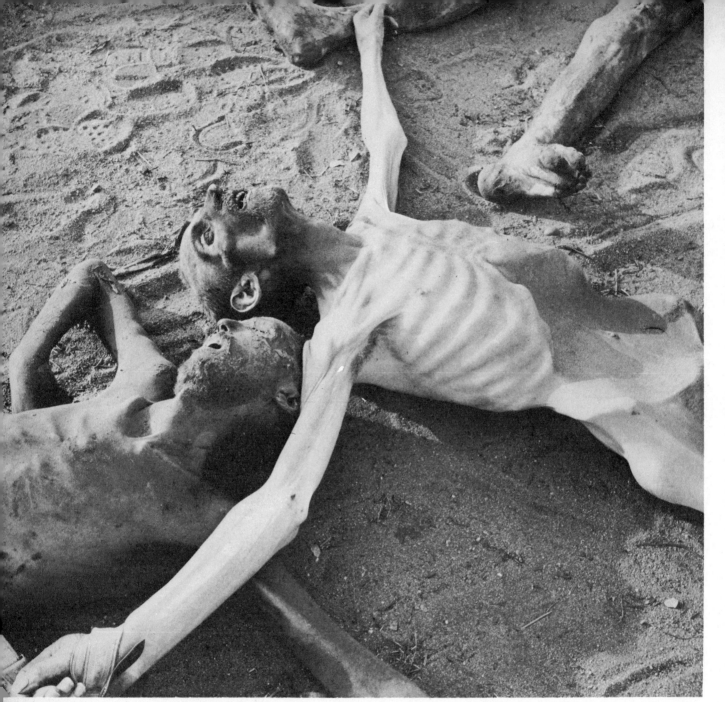

Ecce Homo 1945

Typhus Barrack, Belsen *(right)*

The corpses lay among the living. It was difficult to tell who was dead and who was still alive. We all looked so alike. Bodies so emaciated that they were like skeletons, and that inscrutable, shocked expression in our eyes. Nobody buried the dead. Those who still breathed waited for the miracle, and a ray of hope still flickered in their hearts. Many failed to survive, however, in spite of all their efforts, and died only a few days, often a few hours before the liberation.

196

Statement of Zdenka Vantlova

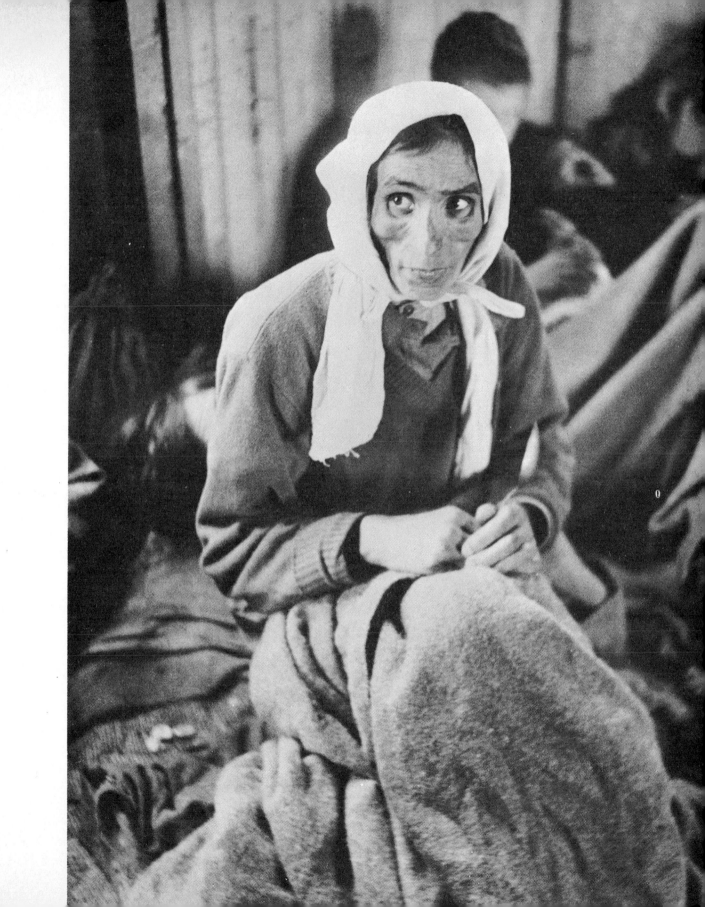

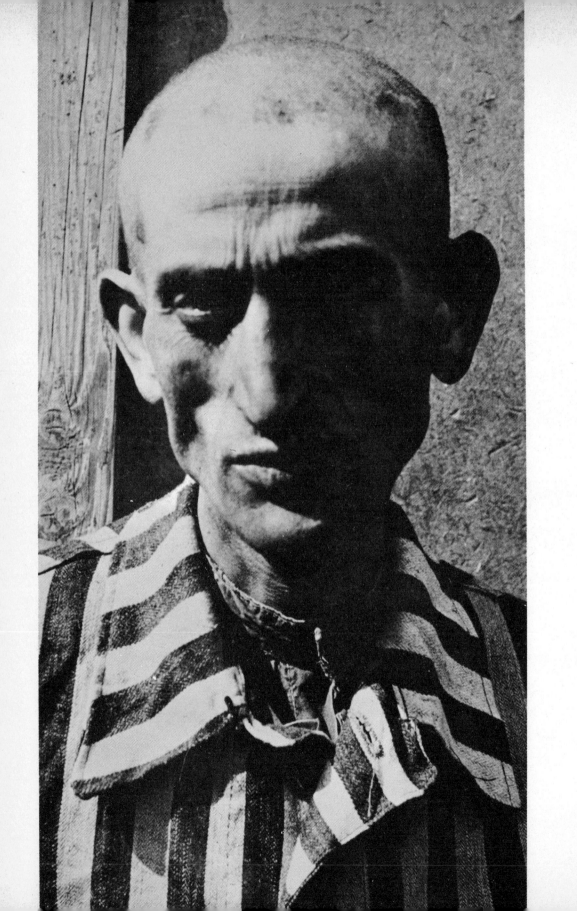

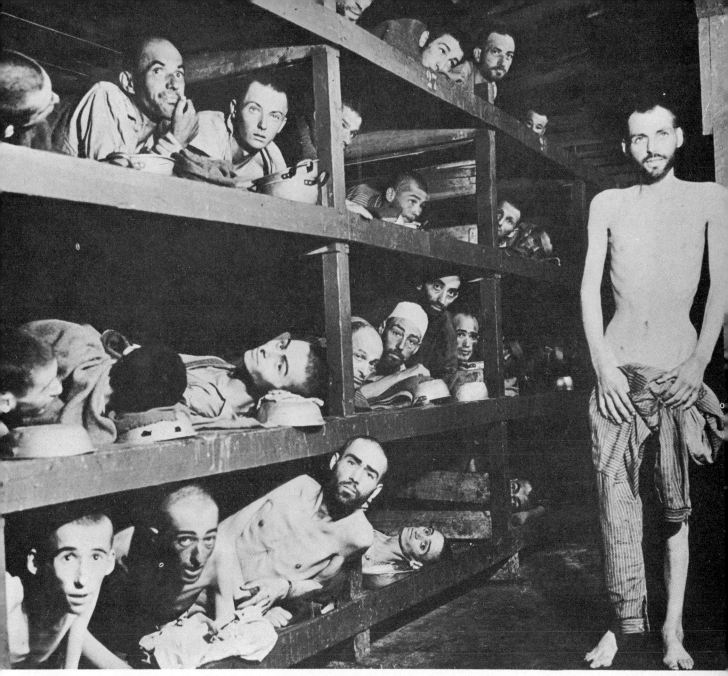

Prisoners in Buchenwald, Dachau *(left)* **and Wobbelin** *(pages 200–1)*

American doctors discovered that the prisoners weighed on an average between 28 and 36 kilogrammes (approx. 4 st. 6 lb. and 5 st. 10 lb.). Most of them had lost 50–60 per cent of their normal weight and had shrunk to less than their normal height. In many cases the harsh imprisonment had caused irreparable physical and mental damage.

Many survivors no longer had the strength to lift themselves up, and lay apathetically in their barracks. The few healthy ones had to help bury their comrades and clear up the camp in order to check the danger of epidemics.

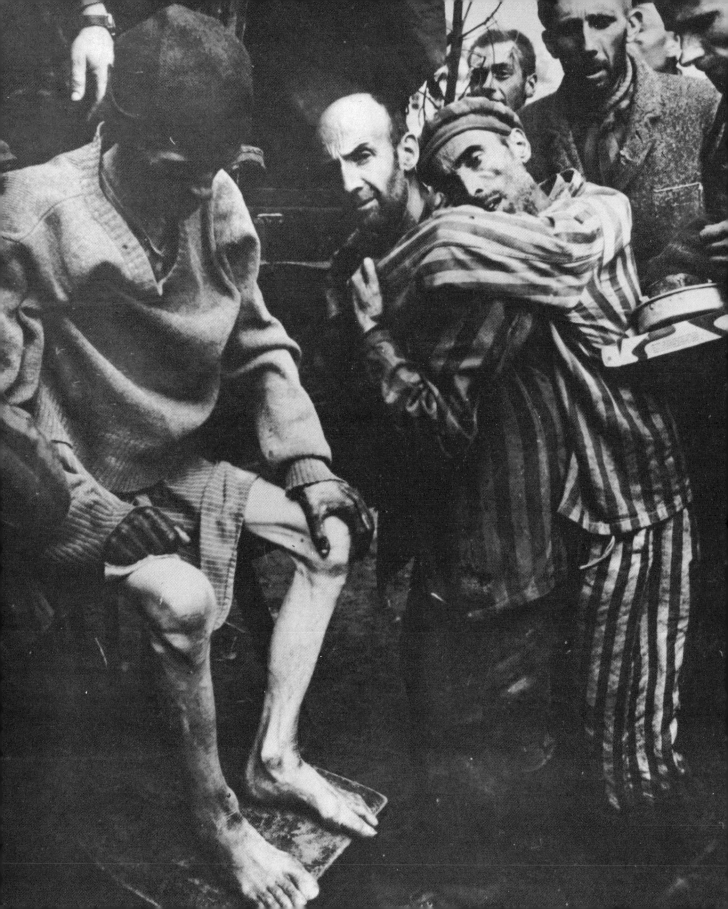

In der Nacht vom 20-21.1.44 aus der Wohnung CC-380
Promenade des Anglais, NYONS - Dröme von der Gestapo
verhaftet und zum Fort Montluc - LYON transportiert

vom 28.1.44 bis 3.2.44 Aufenthalt in Dramcy bei PARIS

ab 3.2.44 deportiert, ohne jede Nachricht.

evtl. Nachrichten an Louis LAZAR, NYONS (Dröme) France.

LAZAR Berthe   LAZAR Ruth   LAZAR Günther
née Salmon   né le 20.4.1926   né le 12.9.1927
né le 5.2.1903

LAZAR Kurt   LAZAR Francine   STRAUSS Werner
né le 27.3.1931   né le 23.6.1930   né le 24.10.1928

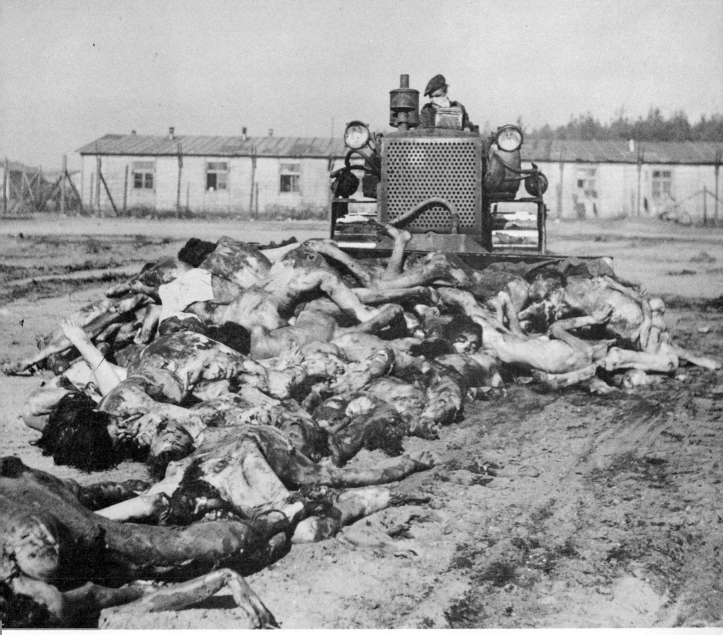

Missing, last seen . . .

The survivors often had to learn that they were the sole remaining members of a large family. Frequently no-one could even tell them when and where their relatives had died. Perhaps they had been burned in Auschwitz years before: perhaps they were among the nameless multitude of dead that British soldiers in Belsen bulldozed by the thousand into huge mass graves. To Dr. Klein, the camp doctor of Belsen, they were all mere vermin (*pages 204–5*).

203

The Female Overseers in Belsen and their Victims

The Principal Accused at Nuremberg

In any war, in this war no doubt there have been—and no doubt on both sides—numbers of brutalities and atrocities. They must have seemed terrible enough to those against whom they were committed. I do not excuse or belittle them. But they were casual, unorganised, individual acts. We are dealing here with something entirely different. With systematic, wholesale, consistent action, taken as a matter of deliberate calculation—calculation at the highest level . . .

There is one group to which the method of annihilation was applied on a scale so immense that it is my duty to refer separately to the evidence. I mean the extermination of the Jews. If there were no other crime against these men, this one alone, in which all of them were implicated, would suffice. History holds no parallel to these horrors.

Sir Hartley Shawcross, British Chief Prosecutor at Nuremberg

Captured SS Guards in Belsen

Who are the guilty ones? Those who ordered the murder, those who carried it out, those who made money out of it, or those who kept quiet about it? The executioners pleaded orders from above, but the leaders of the Third *Reich* could remember nothing. Those who did not escape trial by committing suicide were a sorry sight. For years they had not shrunk from any crime. Now, they all said it was not them.

Goering, who had ordered the "final solution", denied all knowledge of the mass murders. Kaltenbrunner, Heydrich's successor in the RSHA, put all the blame on to the dead Himmler. Ribbentrop, the Foreign Minister, described himself as Hitler's messenger boy, without any influence; Keitel, the Chief of the High Command of the Armed Forces, maintained that he had been led astray; and Streicher, the Party Whip for the anti-Semitic murder campaign, styled himself a harmless writer.

These two-score years in this twentieth century will be recorded in the book of years as some of the most bloody in all annals. Two world wars have left a legacy of dead which number more than all the armies engaged in any war that made ancient or medieval history. No half-century ever witnessed slaughter on such a scale, such cruelties and inhumanities, such wholesale deportations of peoples into slavery, such annihilations of minorities. The terror of Torquemada pales before the Nazi Inquisition.

These deeds are the overshadowing historical facts by which generations to come will remember this decade. If we cannot eliminate the causes and prevent the repetition of these barbaric events, it is not an irresponsible prophecy to say that this twentieth century may yet succeed in bringing the doom of civilisation.

Robert H. Jackson, US Chief Prosecutor at Nuremberg

We waged in many languages the same hard, relentless struggle, a struggle which claimed many victims, and which has not yet ended.

The complete eradication of Nazism is our watchword.

The building of a new world of peace and freedom is our aim.

This we owe to our murdered comrades, and their families.

Oath of the prisoners of Buchenwald, April 1945

212

Epilogue for English readers

This is the book of a German for his fellow-countrymen who, by their action or by default gave the power to a tyrannical government to commit one of the biggest crimes in the history of mankind. The Genocide, the organisation of which is described in this book, is so monstrous, and the thought of moral responsibility for it so intolerable, even for those prepared to try and face it, that any reference to complicity and failure to act on the part of other countries would have provoked the automatic reaction among German readers of ignoring their own conscience and would have prevented the necessary political understanding. That is why this book concentrates on German guilt.

The fact that so many of the Allied and neutral countries did not open their frontiers to the refugees from the Hitler regime while there was still time; that the Swiss authorities suggested that the Nazis should identify the passports of Jews with the letter J, and forcibly rejected the holders of such passports who had fled to their country and sent them back to Germany; that the police apparatus in France and other occupied countries functioned as such perfect executive organs of the Gestapo; that even after the liberation of Rome in Summer 1944, when half a million Hungarian Jews were still being deported to the gas chambers, the Pope could not bring himself to raise his voice publicly against the crime; that no attempt was ever made to destroy the extermination installations of Auschwitz although their exact position and function were known; that not one Statesman on the Allied side took a serious interest in the fate of the Jews because it seemed to have no significance for the outcome of the war: these and similar facts are not mentioned in this book. They have to be taken into account, however, if the bitter truth is to be properly understood.

A German abroad is often asked: "How could this happen? How was it possible in such a civilised nation as Germany?" It is not an easy question to answer.

Anyone who seeks the explanation for Hitler's Third Reich in the German national character and, preaching an inverted racialism, replaces one collective prejudice by another, has ill-learned the lessons of those years. The German people is certainly neither better nor worse than other peoples, even though the failure of a bourgeois-democratic revolution and the century-old tradition of an authoritarian State did produce a specific behaviour pattern that the Nazi dictatorship was able to exploit.

Unquestioning loyalty to any government authority, moral indolence, political opportunism and a concern for personal comfort prevented any humanitarian aid in a situation where it could have been granted without any risk to life and limb.

However, in a regime that declares crime to be law and every humane action to be a crime, the individual can easily find himself in a position where he has only two alternatives—to be either a villain or a hero. And only the very few are born martyrs. Everything therefore depends on creating and maintaining conditions that do not require superhuman efforts to prove one's humanity.

The disturbing question "whether all this only belongs to one country and one time", posed by Cayrol and Resnais in their film "Night and Fog", has long since been answered. Injustice and violence prevail at all points of the compass. "Orders are orders" and "The job has to be done". This type of mentality is not confined to Germany and did not cease to exist in 1945.

The theory of the master race and the practice of terror still serve those in power to maintain established relationships of domination and possession. There still exist racial descent clauses and prohibitive notices excluding men from society by reason of the colour of their skin. There are concentration camps where women and children starve to death in misery; police cells in which men are tortured with electric currents; and a scorched-earth strategy by which an attempt is made to suppress foreign peoples fighting for their independence.

As long as tanks and napalm can be used with impunity to perpetuate the suppression and exploitation of man by man and of one State by another, the spirit of Hitler is still alive.

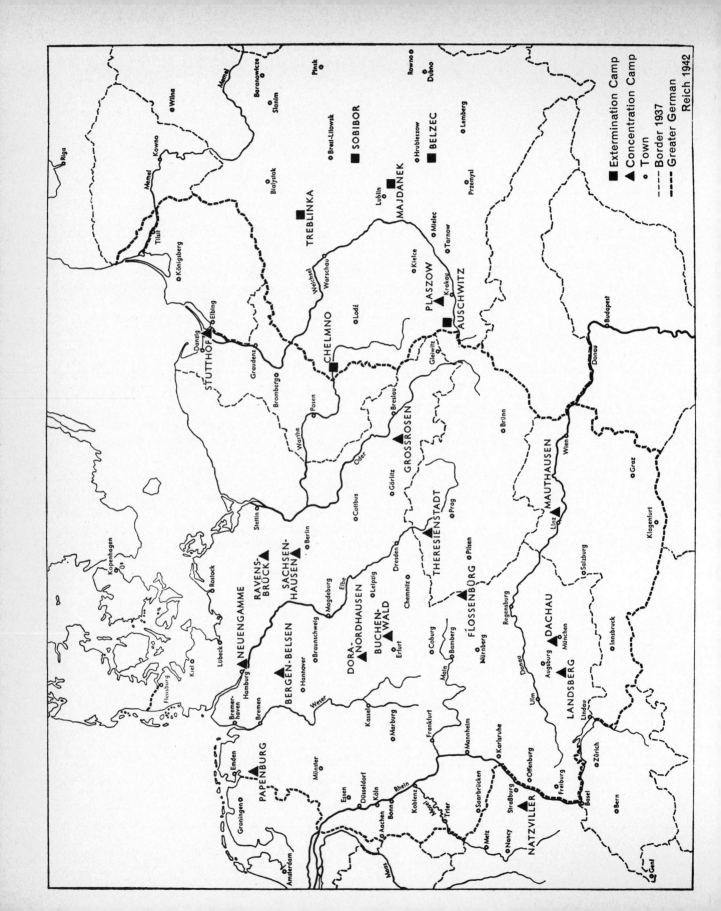

Chronological Table

1933

Jan. 30 President Hindenburg appoints the *"Fuehrer"* of the NSDAP, Adolf Hitler, as *Reich* Chancellor

Feb. 2 Universal ban on demonstrations

24 SA, SS and *Stahlhelm* become "Auxiliary Police"

27 *Reichstag* Fire

28 Mass arrests of Communists. Decree "For the Protection of the People and the State"; suspension of constitutional rights, declaration of State of Emergency (in force until 1945)

Mar. 5 Last General Election to the *Reichstag*; the NSDAP receives 44 per cent of the votes. First "individual acts" against Jewish citizens

23 The *Reichstag* passes the "Enabling Act", with the SPD (Social Democrats) voting against. First concentration camps built

Apr. 1 Boycott by the SA of all Jewish shops and businesses in Germany

7 Law for the Restoration of the professional Civil Service: elimination of all "non-Aryan" civil servants

26 Formation of the *Gestapo* (Secret State Police)

May 2 Dissolution of the free trade unions

10 Burning of books: ban on democratic literature

July 14 One-party State becomes law, political opposition declared punishable by law
Law on the Revocation of Naturalisation and Deprivation of German Citizenship of Jews

Sept. 22 *Reich* Chamber of Culture Law: elimination of Jews

Oct. 4 Editor Law: elimination of Jews

Nov. 12 First General Election in the one-party State: 92 per cent of votes for the NSDAP

Dec. 1 "Unity of Party and State" becomes law

1934

Feb. 7 *Reich* Defence Council decides upon economic preparation for war

June 30
to
July 2 Suppression of "Roehm *Putsch*": the June murders

20 SS becomes an independent organisation

25 Attempted *coup* by the NSDAP in Vienna. Assassination of Austrian Federal Chancellor Dollfuss

Aug. 2 Death of Hindenburg. Hitler becomes Head of State and Commander-in-Chief of the Armed Forces

1935

Jan. 3 Saar plebiscite votes for return to the *Reich*

Mar. 16 Reintroduction of universal conscription

May 21 Military Service Law: "Aryan descent" condition for army service

Summer "No Jews" notices increase in the approaches to towns and villages, outside shops and restaurants

Sept. 15 NSDAP "*Reich* Party Day". Special session of *Reichstag* passes the anti-Semitic Nuremberg Laws: the "*Reich* Citizenship Law" and the "Law for the Protection of German Blood and German Honour"

1936

Mar. 7 Remilitarisation of the Rhineland

29 Public opinion poll: 99 per cent of all votes in favour of Hitler's policy

July 18 Fascist military *coup* against the Spanish Republic: Civil War begins

Aug. 1 Opening of the Olympic Games in Berlin. Temporary removal of anti-Semitic notices

Oct. 25 Formation of the Rome-Berlin Axis

Nov. 25 German-Japanese Anti-Comintern Pact

1937

Nov. 5 Secret meeting in the *Reich* Chancellery: Hitler makes known his war plans

6 Italy joins Anti-Comintern Pact

1938

Mar. 13 *Anschluss* of Austria

28 The Jewish Communities, until now statutory corporations, now become private associations

Apr. 22 Decree against "Camouflage of Jewish Industries"

26 Decree on the Reporting of Jewish Assets: preparation for elimination from the economy

June 14 Decree on the Registration and Identification of Jewish factories

15 Measures against "anti-social" elements: arrest of all "previously convicted" Jews, including those convicted of traffic and similar offences

July 6 Conference of Evian: international conference on the immigration quotas of refugees from Hitler Germany

23 Introduction of identity cards for Jews from 1st January 1939

25 Licences of Jewish doctors expire on 30th September 1938

Aug. 17 Jewish first names (Sara or Israel) proscribed by law as from 1st January 1939

Sept. 27 Compulsory retirement of Jewish lawyers from 30th November

29 Munich Agreement: England and France agree to the annexation of Sudetenland by Hitler

Oct. 5 Passports of Jews are marked with the letter "J"

28 Expulsion of 17,000 "Stateless" Jews out of Germany across the border into Poland

Nov. 7 Herschel Grynszpan, whose parents were deported in the above operation, shoots a member of the German Embassy in Paris, in protest against the injustice

9 "Night of the Broken Glass": State-organised pogrom against Jews in Germany
12 Conference with Goering decides upon "Expiation payment by the Jews" of a thousand million Marks, their elimination from economic life and exclusion from all cultural establishments. Over 26,000 Jewish men arrested and sent to concentration camps
15 Jewish children expelled from schools
28 Introduction of residential restrictions for Jews
Dec. 13 Decree on Compulsory Expropriation ("Aryanisation") of Jewish industries, shops, etc.

1939

Jan. 17 Lifting of tenants' protection from Jews
30 Hitler prophesies in the *Reichstag* "the extermination of the Jewish race in Europe" in the case of war
Mar. 15 German troops march into Czechoslovakia; creation of the "Protectorates of Bohemia and Moravia"
23 German troops march into the Memel District
Apr. 10 Secret report of the *Gestapo* records 302,535 political prisoners in the Third *Reich*
May 18 "*Der Stuermer*" demands the murder of the Jews in the Soviet Union
Aug. 23 German-Soviet Non-Aggression Pact
Sept. 1 German invasion of Poland: the Second World War begins
1–21 SS and *Wehrmacht* organise extensive pogroms in Poland
3 Great Britain and France declare war on Germany
17 Soviet occupation of East Poland
27 Warsaw surrenders
Oct. 12 First deportation of Jews from Austria and Moravia to Poland
28 Jewish star introduced for the first time in Wloclawek, Poland
Nov. 8 Hans Frank appointed *Generalgouverneur* of occupied Poland
Assassination attempt on Hitler in Munich
23 Introduction of Jewish star throughout occupied Poland

1940

Feb. 10–12 First deportations from Stettin, Stralsund and Schneidemuehl to the Lublin district of Poland
Apr. 9 German invasion of Denmark and Norway
30 First ghetto in Lodz
May 10 German invasion of Holland, Belgium and Luxembourg; offensive against France
15 Holland capitulates
28 Belgium capitulates
June 10 Italy enters the war
22 France capitulates
Aug. 15 Eichmann's Madagascar Plan
Sept. 27 Germany-Italy-Japan Tripartite Pact
Oct. 16 Order for the creation of the Warsaw Ghetto
22 "Operation Buerckel": deportation of Jews from Baden, the Palatinate and the Saar

District to the South of France: from there to Auschwitz at the end of 1942
Nov. 15 The Warsaw Ghetto is sealed off

1941

Feb. to
April Deportation of 72,000 Jews to the Warsaw Ghetto
Feb. 22–23 400 Jewish hostages deported from Amsterdam to Mauthausen
Mar. 1 Bulgaria enters the war
7 German Jews used as forced labour
24 Germany invades Africa
Apr. 6 German invasion of Yugoslavia and Greece
17 Yugoslavia capitulates
20 Greece capitulates
May 14 Arrest of 3600 Parisian Jews
End May Formation of the *Einsatzgruppen*
June 22 German invasion of the Soviet Union. Large wave of arrests in Germany
28 Pogrom in Kovno, Lithuania (3800 victims)
July 2/3 Pogrom in Lemberg (7000 victims)
8 Introduction of Jewish star in the Baltic States
11 Massacre in Bialystok
31 Goering charges Heydrich with the evacuation of the European Jews: the "Final Solution" begins
Sept. 15 Introduction of the Jewish star in the German *Reich* for all Jews from the age of 6 years
Sept. 19 Liquidation of the Zhitomir Ghetto, Ukraine (18,000 victims)
23 First gassing experiments in Auschwitz
27 Heydrich becomes *Reich* Protector of Bohemia and Moravia
28/29 Massacre in Kiev (34,000 victims)
Oct. 12/13 Massacre in Dniepropetrovsk (11,000 victims)
14 Order for deportation of German Jews to Lodz: general deportations from the *Reich* begin
End Oct. Massacres in Riga, Vilna, Kovno and Dvinsk
Nov. 6 Mass execution in Rovno (15,000 victims); arrival of first German Jews in Riga, Minsk and Kovno and their execution
25 Decree on the Confiscation of Jewish property on deportation
First massacre in Rostov
Dec. 7 Japanese attack Pearl Harbour: at war with the Allies and the USA
8 Bloodbath of Riga (27,000 victims)
11 Germany declares war on USA
22 Bloodbath of Vilna (32,000 victims)
30 Bloodbath of Simferopol, Crimea (10,000 victims)
End Dec. Permanent extermination camp built at Chelmno

1942

Jan. 15 "Resettlement" of the Lodz Ghetto begins: transportation to Chelmno
20 Heydrich's Wannsee Conference on the so-called "Final Solution of the Jewish question" in Europe
31 Report of *Einsatzgruppe A* on the liquidation of 229,052 Jews in the Baltic States

End Jan. Beginning of deportations to Theresienstadt
Feb./Mar. Mass murder of Jews in Kharkov (14,000 victims)
Mar. 16 Belsec extermination camp built
17—21 "Resettlement" of Lublin Ghetto: transportation to Belsec, Maidanek and other camps (26,000 people)
28 The first Slovak Jews arrive in the Auschwitz-Birkenau camp
First Paris-Auschwitz transport
April—July "Resettlement" extends over the whole of Poland
New transports of Jews from the German *Reich* to the Polish death camps
Apr. 26 The *Reichstag* ratifies Hitler's suspension of the legal system
May 18 Sobibor extermination camp built in the Lublin district
27 Assassination of Heydrich in Prague by Czech patriots
June 1 Introduction of the Jewish star in France and Holland
23 First selection for the gas chamber in Auschwitz
July Massacres in Minsk, Lida, Slonim and Rovno
15 First deportation train from Holland to Auschwitz
Large-scale police raid in Paris
22 Warsaw "resettlement" begins: transportation to the Belsec and Treblinka concentration camps
Aug. 4 First deportation from Belgium to Auschwitz
10—22 "Resettlement" of Lemberg Ghetto
Mid-Aug. German troops in the Caucasus
26—28 Arrest of 7000 Stateless Jews in unoccupied France
Aug./Sept. Deportations from Zagreb, Croatia, to Auschwitz;
Jews deported from Theresienstadt gassed in Minsk, Byelorussia
Sept. 9 Massacre in Kislovodsk, Caucasus
16 "Resettlement" of Lodz Ghetto completed (55,000 victims)
30 Hitler publicly repeats his prophecy on the extermination of Jewry
Oct. 3 First "resettlement" of Warsaw Ghetto completed (310,000 people)
4 The concentration camps in Germany become "Jew-free": all Jewish prisoners go to Auschwitz
18 The Reich Ministry of Justice delegates to the Gestapo responsibility for Jews and Poles in the *Reich*
28 First part of "*Einsatz Reinhard*" completed. More than 50 ghettos in Poland
Oct. 29 Mass execution of Jews in Pinsk, Byelorussia (16,000 victims)
Nov. 7 Allied landings in North Africa
22 Start of the Soviet counter-offensive
25 First deportations of Jews from Norway to Auschwitz
Dec. 17 The Allies solemnly promise that the extermination of Jews will be expiated

1943

Jan. 18 First resistance to deportations in the Warsaw Ghetto

20—26 Transports from the Theresienstadt Ghetto to Auschwitz
Feb. 2 The German Sixth Army surrenders at Stalingrad
5—12 First "resettlement" in Bialystok
27 Deportation of Jewish armament workers from Berlin to Auschwitz
Mar. Transports from Holland to Sobibor; from Prague, Vienna, Luxembourg and Macedonia to Treblinka
Mar./May Second "resettlement" in Croatia
Mar. 13 Crackow Ghetto broken up
The first of the new crematoria in Auschwitz opened
Attempted assassination of Hitler by officers of the Central Army Group in the Soviet Union
15 Deportations from Salonika and Thrace
19 Bermuda Conference: International conference on immigration quotas for refugees from Hitler-occupied Europe
Apr. 19/May 16 Uprising and destruction of the Warsaw Ghetto
May 9 Surrender of the last German-Italian armed forces in North Africa
June 11 Himmler orders the liquidation of all Polish ghettos; decree extended to the Soviet Union on the 21st
21—27 Liquidation of the Lemberg Ghetto (20,000 people)
25 Uprising and destruction of the Czenstochowa Ghetto
9 Allied landings in Sicily
Aug. 2 Uprising in Treblinka
Aug. Exhumation operation in Kiev and the death camps after the advance of the Soviet troops
16—23 Uprising and destruction of the Bialystok Ghetto
Sept. 8 Italy signs armistice with the Allies. German troops occupy North and Central Italy
11 Beginning of German police raids on Jews in Nice
11—14 Liquidation of ghettos in Minsk and Lida
11—18 "Family transports" from Theresienstadt to Auschwitz
23 Liquidation of the Vilna Ghetto
25 Soviet troops recapture Smolensk. Liquidation of all ghettos in Byelorussia
Oct. 13 Italy declares war on Germany
14 Uprising in Sobibor
18 First Rome-Auschwitz transport of Jews
Nov. 3 Liquidation of the Riga Ghetto
Murder of the remaining Jews in the Maidanek concentration camp (17,000)
6 Kiev recaptured by Soviet troops
28 Teheran Conference
Dec. 15—19 First trial of German war criminals in Kharkov

1944

Mar. 15 Soviet troops cross the River Bug
28 Soviet troops in Galicia
Apr. 10 Transnistrien, Bukowina and Bessarabia liberated
14 First Athens-Auschwitz transports of Jews
May 15—July 8 476,000 Jews deported from Hungary to Auschwitz

June 4 Allies in Rome
6 Beginning of Allied invasion
23 Soviet offensive starts
July 20 Attempted assassination of Hitler. Mass arrests and executions
24 Soviet troops liberate the Maidanek concentration camp
25 Kovno Ghetto evacuated
Aug. 6 27,000 Jews deported to Germany from camps east of the River Vistula
23 Assembly camp of Drancy (Paris) liberated Rumania capitulates
Sept. 5 Lodz Ghetto evacuated
11 British troops reach Holland
13 Soviet troops on the Slovak border
Sept. Deportation of all Jews in Dutch camps to Germany. New deportations from Theresienstadt to Auschwitz. Last transport from France to Auschwitz
14 US troops on the German border
23 Bloodbath in the Kluga camp, Estonia Resumption of deportations from Slovakia
Oct. 7 Attempted outbreak in Auschwitz-Birkenau
18 Hitler orders the setting-up of the *Volkssturm*
End Oct. The survivors of the Plaszow (Crackow) concentration camp transported to Auschwitz Last gassings in Auschwitz
Nov. Trial of the staff of the Maidanek extermination camp in Lublin
Nov. 3 Soviet troops outside Budapest
8–18 Eichmann deports 38,000 Jews from Budapest to the concentration camps of Buchenwald, Ravensbrueck, etc.
26 Himmler orders the destruction of the crematoria in Auschwitz-Birkenau

1945

Jan. 16 Soviet troops liberate 800 Jews in Czenstochowa and 870 in Lodz
17 Liberation of 80,000 Jews in Budapest
26 Auschwitz liberated by Soviet troops
Feb. 4 Yalta Conference in the Crimea
Mar. 5 US troops on the Rhine
19 Hitler orders the destruction of the whole of Germany
Apr. 6–10 Evacuation of 15,000 Jews from Buchenwald
11 Buchenwald liberated by US troops
15 Bergen-Belsen concentration camp liberated by British troops
20 US troops in Nuremberg
23 Mauthausen taken over by the International Red Cross
Soviet troops outside Berlin
23–May 4 Evacuation of prisoners from Sachsenhausen (Berlin) and Ravensbrueck. Last massacre by the SS guards
25 Meeting of US and Soviet troops on the Elbe
28 Dachau liberated by US troops
30 Hitler commits suicide
May 2 Berlin surrenders
7 Germany's unconditional surrender End of war in Europe
10 Theresienstadt liberated
23 Himmler commits suicide
June 26 Foundation of the United Nations
Aug. 6 First atom bomb on Hiroshima
15 Japan surrenders
End of the Second World War
Nov. 22 Beginning of Nuremberg Trial

Sources of Text

In the interests of readability and in order to include as much information as possible in the available space, the amount of textual material relating to a particular event had to be severely limited. Unless otherwise stated, the official documents and eye-witness accounts reproduced in this book are extracts. The sources, where the complete documents may be found, are given below.

The following abbreviations have been used for the institutes where the documents are to be found:

CDJC Centre de Documentation Juive Contemporaine. Paris
RvO Rijksinstituut voor Oorlogsdocumentatie, Amsterdam
WL The Wiener Library, Institute of Contemporary History, London
YW Yad Washem, Jerusalem
ZIH Zydowski Instytut Historyczny, Warsaw

5 Bertolt Brecht, *Hundert Gedichte 1918–1950*, Berlin 1951. p. 255
10 1. *Der Stuermer*. January 1935, No. 2, p. 5
    2. Arthur D. Morse, *While Six Million Died*, London 1968, p. 212
11 1. *Reichsgesetzblatt*, 1935, Part I, No. 100, p. 1146 f.
    2. Stuckart/Globke, *Kommentare zur deutschen Rassegesetzgebung*, Vol. I, Munich and Berlin 1936, p. 9 ff.
12 1. Secret teleprinter message from the Gestapo dated 9.11.1938; *Dokumente zur Reichskristallnacht*, supplement to the weekly "*Das Parlament*", p. 581
    2. Report of execution of order by SA-Brigade 50, Darmstadt, dated 11.11.1938, PS-1721; International Military Tribunal = IMT, *The Trial of the Major War Criminals before the International Military Tribunal*, Nuremberg 1947–49, Vol. XXVII, p. 487
    3. Report of execution of order by *SS-Sturm* 10/25, Geldern, dated 14.11.1938; N. Blumental (ed.), *Slowa niewinne*, Centralna Zydowska Komisja Historyczna w Polsce, Crackow-Lodz-Warsaw 1947, p. 37
13 Alfred Rosenberg, *Der Mythus des 20. Jahrhunderts*, Munich 1930, p. 670
14 *Vossische Zeitung*, 4.3.1933, in: *Das Schwarzbuch*, Facts and documents—the position of Jews in Germany 1933, ed. by *Comité des Délégations Juives*, Paris 1934, p. 58
17 *Voelkischer Beobachter*, 3.4.1933, in: *Das Schwarzbuch* (see above), p. 65
19 1. Heinrich Heine, *Almansor*, in: Ernst Elster (ed.), *Heines Werke, Bibliographisches Institut Leipzig*, no date, Vol. III, p. 197
    2. *Frankfurter Zeitung*, in: *Das Schwarzbuch* (see above), p. 438
20 Westdeutscher Beobachter, 17.8.1935 (WL)
23 PS-1816; *Dokumente zur Reichskristallnacht* (see p. 12/1), p. 587
30 Express letter from the Chief of the SIPO and SD dated 21.9.1939, PS-3363; T. Berenstein, A. Eisenbach, A. Rutkowski (ed.), *Eksterminacja Zydow na Ziemiach Polskich, Zydowski Instytut Historyczny*, Warsaw 1957, p. 21 f.
31 Introduction of Compulsory Identification of Jews in Crackow, dated 18.11.1939; poster (ZIH)
32 David Rubinowicz, Diary, in: *Polen von heute*, No. 4–6/1960, p. 15.
33 Adolf Hitler, *Mein Kampf*, 40th edition, Munich 1933, p. 742
42 Order dated 3.3.1941 (ZIH, Poster No. 78); Berenstein *inter alia* (see p. 30), p. 111

43 Order dated 2.10.1940; Berenstein *inter alia* (see p. 30), p. 95
44 Teleprinter message No. 161 dated 10.3.1942, Dr. J. Kermisz (ed.), *Dokumenty i Materialy do Dziejow Okupacji Niemieckiej w Polsce*, Vol. II, "*Akcje*" i "*Wysiedlenia*", Centralna Zydowska Komisja Historyczna w Polsce, Warsaw-Lodz-Crackow 1946, p. 24
45 Teleprinter message No. 258 dated 13.3.1942, Kermisz (see above), p. 28
47 The Rev. G. Schedler, Ein Ghetto im Schatten, in: *Friede ueber Israel*, Munich, No. 3, July 1951
48 Josef Wulf, *Vom Leben, Kampf und Tod im Ghetto Warschau*, Supplement to the weekly "*Das Parlament*", p. 167
50 1. Circular letter dated 10.12.1939, Berenstein *inter alia* (see p. 30), p. 77 ff.
    2. Report dated 20.1.1941, Stroop Trial, Vol. 2, 209 ff.; Berenstein *inter alia* (see p. 30), p. 102 ff.
    3. Report dated 26.9.41 (ZIH, K-0100); Berenstein *inter alia* (see p. 30), p. 131 ff.
51 Ludwik Hirszfeld, *Die Stadt des Todes*, Ms. (WL)
52 1. Blumental (see p. 12/3), p. 179
    2. Blumental (see p. 12/3), p. 180
    3. A. Eisenbach (ed.), *Dokumenty i Materialy*, Vol. III, *Getto Lodzkie, Centralna Zydowska Komisja Historyczna w Polsce*, Warsaw-Lodz-Crackow 1946, p. 86 f.
53 1. Telegram dated 24.12.1941 (ZIH K-2600); Berenstein *inter alia* (see p. 30), p. 167 f.
    2. Kermisz (see p. 44), p. 194
    3. Blumental (see p. 12/3), p. 83
    4. Kermisz (see p. 44), p. 169
    5. Blumental (see p. 12/3), p. 80
54 1. Sworn affidavit of building engineer Hermann Friedrich Graebe in Wiesbaden on 10.11.1945, PS-2992: IMT (see p. 12/2), Vol. XXXI, pp. 443–4
    2. Bernard Goldstein, *The Stars bear Witness*, New York 1949, p. 145
55 Announcement No. 428 concerning the beginning of the evacuation of Lodz Ghetto, dated 22.8.1944; Poster (WL)
56 1. Letter from M. Tennenbaum, commander of the ghetto uprising in Bialystok; Wulf (see p. 48), p. 174
    2. *The Black Book of Polish Jewry*, pub. by the American Federation of Polish Jews, New York 1943, p. 134
57 Circular letter from Uebelhoer, District President of Kalisch, dated 10.12.1939; Berenstein *inter alia* (see p. 30), p. 80
58 Blumental (see p. 12/2), p. 98

63 W. Szpilman in: Wulf (see page 48), p. 168

65 Dr. Freiherr du Prel, *Das deutsche Generalgouverne-ment Polen*, Crackow 1940, p. 143, in: Poliakov/ Wulf II (ed.), *Das Dritte Reich und seine Diener*, Berlin 1956, p. 384

70 *Generalgouverneur* Hans Frank on 9.9.1941; Poliakov/Wulf I (ed.), *Das Dritte Reich und die Juden*, Berlin 1955, p. 177

72 Blumental (see p. 12/3), p. 181

73 Appeal "*An die Einwohner des juedischen Wohn-bezirks*" in Warsaw on 1.8.1942; T. Berenstein, A. Eisenbach, B. Mark, A. Rutkowski (ed.), *Faschismus—Getto—Massenmord*, Berlin 1960, p. 309

74 Alfred Goldstein (ed.), *Cinq récits des enfants du ghetto*, London, no date, p. 22

75 Poster (ZIH)

76 Report dated 24.9.1942; Blumental (see p. 12/3), p. 137

77 Note dated 17.3.1942 on a conversation with *SS-Hauptsturmfuehrer* Hoefle, Lublin; Kermisz (see p. 44), p. 32

78 Trial IV, p. 2184 f. of the German transcript, in: Gerald Reitlinger, *Die Endloesung*, Berlin 1956, p. 288

80 *Goebbels-Tagebuecher*, Zurich 1948, p. 142 f.

82 1. Report to General Thomas dated 2.12.1941. PS-3257; Poliakov/Wulf II (see p. 65), p. 521
   2. Secret progress report of *Einsatzgruppe* A for the period 16.10.1941 to 31.1.1942, PS-2273; IMT (see p. 12/2), Vol. XXX, p. 72 ff.
   3. Report to the *Reichskommissar fuer das Ostland,* Hinrich Lohse, Riga, dated 31.7.1942 (photostat WL)

83 Affidavit Graebe (see p. 54/1). Vol. XIX, pp. 507—9

84 Affidavit Metzner NO-5558 (WL)

85 Report on the execution of Jews and gipsies, NOKW 905; Jewish Museum, Belgrade

88 (CDJC); see also Poliakov/Wulf I (see p. 70), p. 383

92 Lecture note, 6.2.1940, (CDJC); see also Polia-kov/Wulf II (see p. 65), p. 516

93 Himmler's speech in Poznan on 4.10.1943, PS-1919; *Das Urteil im Wilhelmstrassen-Prozess*, Schwaebisch-Gmuend 1950, p. 114

95 Poliakov/Wulf II (see p. 65), p. 405

97 R-135; Poliakov/Wulf I (see p. 70)

102 1. Proclamation on the registration of the Jews in The Hague, Holland, dated 31.1.1941; poster (photo RvO)
   2. Proclamation on the registration of the Jews in Belgrade, Yugoslavia, dated 16.4.1941; poster (photo Jewish Museum, Belgrade)
   3. Proclamation on the registration of the Jews in Vichy, France, dated 24.7.1941; poster (photo Stephane Richter, Paris)

103 1. NG-2586-E; (photostat RvO)
   2. Transcript dated 20.1.1942, NG-2586-G (photostat RvO)

104 Circular letter dated 20.3.1942, Duesseldorf Gestapo papers (photostat WL)

105 Report dated 26.12.1941, Duesseldorf Gestapo papers (photostat WL)

106 NG-2631 (photostat RvO)

107 1—4. CDJC
   5. Georges Wellers, *De Drancy à Auschwitz*, Paris 1946, p. 58

108 1. (photostat RvO)

2. Poliakov/Wulf II (see p. 70), p. 85

113 *Reichsgesetzblatt*, Vol. 1941, Part I, No. 100, p. 547

114 Express letter dated 22.6.1942, (photostat RvO)

116 Dutch underground leaflet (RvO)

118 Report by Police Inspector Stecker dated 9.3.1942 on a meeting in the RSHA, Dept.IV B 4, on 6.3.1942, Duesseldorf Gestapo Papers (photostat WL)

122 *Commandant in Auschwitz*, the autobiography of Rudolf Hoess, London 1959, p. 184

123 Teleprinter message dated 29.4.1943 (CDJC)

124 Letter dated 30.7.1942 (CDJC)

132 The *Reichsfuehrer SS* to the Chief of the SIPO and the SD on 9.4.1943 (photostat RvO)

134 *Vierteljahreshefte fuer Zeitgeschichte*, 1st vol.1953, 2nd No., April, p. 185 ff.

136 PS-3868; IMT (see p. 12/2), Vol. XXXIII, pp. 275—8

137 Diary of *SS-Hauptsturmfuehrer* Prof. Dr. med. Johann Kremer (Auschwitz Museum)

138 1. Statement of former prisoner, mathematics student Kai Feinberg, Oslo, at the Nuremberg Trial; *SS im Einsatz*, Berlin 1957, p. 464
   2. Statement of former prisoner Prof. Marc Klein, Strassburg; Poliakov/Wulf I (see p. 70), p. 253 f.
   3. Statement of former prisoner Marie Claude Vaillant-Couturier, Deputy, Paris, at the Nuremberg Trial; IMT (see p. 12/2), Vol. VI, pp. 206—7
   4. Statement of former prisoner Noack Treister, Prague, at the Nuremberg Trial; *SS im Einsatz* (see above), p. 472
   5. Statement of former prisoner Grégoire Afrine, Paris, at the Nuremberg Trial; *SS im Einsatz* (see above), p. 458
   6. Statement of former prisoner Dr. Robert Levy, Strassburg; Poliakov/Wulf I (see p. 70), p. 264

139 1. NI-11118; Reimund Schnabel, *Macht ohne Moral*, Frankfurt 1957, p. 227
   2. NI-4033; see also Hellwig Deicke, *Ein Tagebuch fuer Anne Frank*, Berlin, no date
   3. *SS im Einsatz* (see p. 138/1), p. 466 f.
   4. *SS im Einsatz* (see p. 138/1), p. 455
   5. *SS im Einsatz* (see p. 138/1), p. 469

140 1. Teleprinter message dated 16.12.1942, PS-1472; IMT (see p. 12/2), Vol. XXVII, p. 251
   2. Morse (see p.11/2), p.53

142 Statement at the Nuremberg Trial; *SS im Einsatz* (see p. 138/1), p. 268

143 Giza Landau, *Im Lager*; Poliakov/Wulf I (see p. 70), p. 286

144 Hoess (see p. 136),

145 Gerstein (see p. 134)

146 Hoess (see p. 122), p. 194—195

148 Dr. Ella Lingens-Reiner, *Prisoners of Fear*, London 1948, p. 70

161 *SS-Untersturmfuehrer* Schwarz, Auschwitz Con-centration Camp, to the *Hauptamt Haushalt und Bauten*, Berlin-Lichterfelde, Unter den Eichen 126; Blumental (see p. 12/3), p. 181

164 Hitler speech on 8.11.1942, in: *Deutschland im zweiten Weltkrieg*, original recordings from the years 1939 to 1945 (2 long-playing records) Ariola, Guetersloh

166 Daily reports of *SS-Brigadefuehrer und General-leutnant der Polizei* Juergen Stroop. to the *Hoehere SS- und Polizeifuehrer Ost*, Crackow, in "*Es gibt*

keinen juedischen Wohnbezirk in Warschau mehr", report on the liquidation of the Warsaw Ghetto dated 16.5.1943, PS-1061; IMT (see p. 12/2), Vol. XXXVI, p. 628 f.

169 Bernard Mark, *Der Aufstand im Warschauer Ghetto*, Berlin 1959, p. 384

170 Introduction to the Stroop Report (see p. 166)

174 Introduction to the Stroop Report (see p. 166)

175 Mark (see p. 169), p. 316

177 Introduction to the Stroop Report (see p. 166)

178 Cywia Lubetkin, *Die letzten Tage des Warschauer Ghettos*; Commentary, New York, May 1947

180 Appeal of the ZZW (Jewish Fighter Organisation) dated 22.1.1943 (ZIH, *Archiv Ringelblum* II No.333/3); Mark (see p. 169), p. 171

181 Last report received from the ZOB dated 26.4.1943; Mark (see p. 169), p. 337

182 P. Elster, Notes; Mark (see p. 169), p. 317

183 Letter dated 1.3.1944 to New York; Wulf (see p. 48), p. 171

186 1. *SS im Einsatz* (see p. 138/1), p. 235 f.

2. *Témoignages Strasbourgeois*, Paris 1954, p. 90

3. Grete Salus, *Eine Frau erzaehlt*, series of the *Bundeszentrale fuer Heimatdienst*, Part 36, Bonn 1958, p. 77

4. *SS im Einsatz* (see p. 138/1), p. 232

187 1. *SS im Einsatz* (see p. 138/1), p. 250

2. *SS im Einsatz* (see p. 138/1), p. 190

188 1. PS-2738; Poliakov/Wulf I (see p. 70), p. 99

2. IMT (see p. 12/2), Vol. IV, p. 371

190 Order from the *Reichsfuehrer SS* dated 4.4.1945 to the Camp Commandants of Dachau and Flossenbuerg; Blumental (see p. 12/3), p. 236

193 Eugen Kogan, *Heute*, Munich 1946, No. 3

196 Zdenka Vantlova, *Modernes Mittelalter*, Ms. (YW E/1–4–1)

208 Concluding speech by prosecution at the Nuremberg Trial, IMT, Vol. XIX, pp. 467, and 501

211 Concluding speech by prosecution at the Nuremberg Trial, IMT, Vol. XIX, p. 397

212 *Buchenwald—Mahnung und Verpflichtung*, Berlin 1960, p. 563

Sources of Photographs

The majority of illustrations are reproduced from photographs taken at the instance or with the permission of the Nazi authorities. Some of the illustrations of the Warsaw Ghetto and those of the registration of Russian Jews in Odessa come from large series of official photographs taken by the German "Propaganda Companies". The amateur photographs of a mass execution in Latvia were also found in an abandoned Gestapo office.

The photographs of the deportations in Holland are taken from a series that the commanders of the Security Police and Security Service ordered to be prepared. The pictures of the arrival and selection of deportees in Auschwitz-Birkenau come from a collection of over 200 photographs that were taken by an SS officer in summer 1944 as the mass transports arrived from Hungary. The photographs of the Warsaw Ghetto uprising represent a selection from a total of 53 photographs in an illustrated report on the event prepared by the SS. The other pictures are private photographs that were confiscated from captured servicemen and SS men, or photographs taken secretly by members of the Resistance Movement. The photographs from the Imperial War Museum, London, are an exception. These were taken by Press photographers with the Allied forces after the liberation of the concentration camps.

Allgemeine Wochenzeitung der Juden in Deutschland, Duesseldorf: 40 (2)

Associated Press, Frankfort: 160 bot., 163 (4), 192

Bundesarchiv Koblenz: 34, 58, 59, 60 (2), 61, 63, 66, 68, 69, 70, 74, 75

CAF, Warsaw: 152 top, 152 (2), 155 top

Centre de Documentation Juive Contemporaine, Paris: 36, 38 top, 42, 43, 44, 45, 72/73, 76, 77, 79 top, 79 bot., 80, 88, 89 bot., 92, 93, 98, 109, 118, 124, 126 (2), 127, 128, 155 bot., 158 (2), 189, 194, 202

Hoffmann-Archiv, Munich: 46, 47

Deutsche Presse-Agentur, Frankfort: 190

Imperial War Museum, London: 160 top, 161, 163 (5), 191, 193, 196, 197, 198, 199, 203, 204/205, 206, 207, 209, 210, 211, 212

Keystone, Munich: 21

Kongress-Verlag, Berlin: 15, 22, 39 top, 64 top, 65, 71

Landesbildstelle Berlin: 16

Alfred Merges, Zittau: 14

Jevrejski muzej, Belgrade: 38 bot., 208

National Archives, Washington D.C.: 17, 200, 201 (2)

Panstwowe Muzeum, Auschwitz: 141, 152 bot., 156 (2), 157 (2), 162 (2), 164, 195 (3)

Rijksinstituut voor Oorlogsdocumentatie, Amsterdam: 20, 25, 110/111 (9), 112, 113, 114, 115 (2), 116, 117, 122, 123, 125, 129, 130 (2), 131 (2), 132

Roederberg Verlag, Frankfort: 86/87 (4)

Ruetten und Loening, Berlin: 35 top, 41

Statni zidovske muzeum, Prague: 142, 143, 144, 145, 146, 147, 148, 149, 154

Stern Magazin, Hamburg: 163 (3)

Glavnoye arkhivnoye upravleniye, Moscow: 90/91 (4), 94, 95, 96/97 (5), 99 (2), 100, 159

Ullstein, Berlin: 13, 18/19, 26, 27

The Wiener Library, Institute of Contemporary History, London: 23, 24, 28

Yad Washem, Jerusalem: 67, 85

Zentralbild, Berlin: 150/151

Zydowski Instytut Historyczny, Warsaw: 33, 35 bot., 37, 39 bot., 48, 57, 62, 64 bot., 78, 89 top, 119, 120/121 (4), 163 (1), 163 (2), 169–184 (18)

Bibliography

History and Analysis of Anti-Semitism

Paul W. Massing: *Rehearsal for Destruction*. A study of political anti-Semitism in Imperial Germany (1870–1918), Harper & Bros., New York 1949, 341 pp.
Eva G. Reichmann: *Hostages of Civilisation*. The sources of National-Socialist anti-Semitism, Gollancz, London 1950, 281 pp.
Hannah Arendt: *The Origins of Totalitarianism*. Allen & Unwin, London, 1958, 520 pp.
Jean-Paul Sartre: *Betrachtungen zur Judenfrage. Psychoanalyse des Antisemitismus*, Europa Verlag, Zurich 1948, 135 pp.
Theodor W. Adorno and others: *The Authoritarian Personality*. Harper & Bros., New York 1950, 990 pp.
Cyril Bibby: *Race, Prejudice and Education*. Heinemann, London 1959, 90 pp.

Nazi System

Alan Bullock: *Hitler. A Study in Tyranny* (compl. rev. ed.), Odhams Press, London 1964, 848 pp.
William Shirer: *The Rise and Fall of the Third Reich*. A history of Nazi Germany, Secker & Warburg, London 1960, 1245 pp.
Edward Crankshaw: *Gestapo. Instrument of Tyranny*, Putnam, London 1956, 275 pp.
Eugen Kogon: *The Theory and Practice of Hell*. The German concentration camps and the system behind them, Secker and Warburg, London 1950, 307 pp.
Reinhard Henkys: *Die nationalsozialistischen Gewaltverbrechen, Geschichte und Gericht*, Kreuz-Verlag, Stuttgart/Berlin 1964, 392 pp.
Walther Hofer: *Der Nationalsozialismus*. Dokumente 1933–1945, S. Fischer Verlag, Frankfurt a.M. 1957, 385 pp.
Reimund Schnabel (ed.): *Macht ohne Moral. Eine Dokumentation ueber die SS*, Roederberg Verlag, Frankfurt a.M. 1957, 580 pp.
Alexander Mitscherlich/Fred Mielke (eds.): *The Death Doctors*. Elek Books, London 1962, 367 pp.

Persecution of Jews

(a) General
Gerald Reitlinger: *The Final Solution*. The attempt to exterminate the Jews of Europe, Vallentine & Mitchell, London 1968, 668 pp.
Raoul Hilberg: *The Destruction of the European Jews*. Quadrangle Books, Chicago 1967, 790 pp.
Wolfgang Scheffler: *Judenverfolgung im Dritten Reich 1933–1945*. Buechergilde Gutenberg, Frankfurt a.M. 1961, 245 pp.
H. G. Adler: *Theresienstadt 1941–1945. Das Antlitz einer Zwangsgemeinschaft*, J. C. B. Mohr, Tuebingen 1955, 773 pp.

(b) Documentation
H. G. Adler (ed.): *Die verheimlichte Wahrheit. Theresienstaedter Dokumente*, J. C. B. Mohr, Tuebingen 1958, 372 pp.
Léon Poliakov/Josef Wulf (eds.): *Das Dritte Reich und die Juden*. Dokumente und Aufsaetze, arani, Berlin 1955, 457 pp.
Léon Poliakov/Josef Wulf (eds.): *Das Dritte Reich und seine Diener*. Dokumente, arani, Berlin 1956, 540 pp.
Bruno Blau: *Das Ausnahmerecht fuer die Juden in Deutschland 1933–1945* (mimeogr.), New York 1952, 144 pp.
Commandant of Auschwitz. The autobiography of Rudolf Hoess, Weidenfeld & Nicolson, London 1959, 252 pp.

(c) Eye-witness Accounts
The Black Book. The Nazi crime against the Jewish people, The Jewish Black Book Committee, New York 1946, 560 pp.
Eric H. Boehm (ed.): *We survived*. The stories of fourteen of the hidden and hunted of Nazi Germany, Yale University Press, New Haven 1949, 308 pp.
Philip Friedman (ed.): *Martyrs and Fighters* (anthology on the Warsaw Ghetto), Praeger, New York 1954, 254 pp.
Olga Wormser/Henri Michel (eds.): *Tragédie de la déportation 1940–1945. Témoignages de survivants des camps de concentration allemands*, Hachette, Paris 1955, 511 pp.
Im Feuer vergangen. Tagebuecher aus dem Ghetto, Ruetten & Loening, Berlin 1958, 608 pp.
De l'Université aux Camps de Concentration. Témoignages Strasbourgeois, Les Belles Lettres, Paris 1954, 560 pp.
H. G. Adler/Hermann Langbein/Ella Lingens-Reiner (eds.): *Auschwitz, Zeugnisse und Berichte*, Europaeische Verlagsanstalt, Frankfurt a.M. 1962, 423 pp.
Gerhard Schoenberner (ed.): *Wir haben es gesehen. Augenzeugenberichte ueber die Judenverfolgung im Dritten Reich*, Ruetten & Loening, Hamburg 1962, 430 pp.

Resistance

Helmut Gollwitzer (ed.): *Dying we live*. The final messages and records of the Resistance, Pantheon, New York 1956, 285 pp.
Phillip Friedman: *Their Brothers' Keepers*. The Christian heroes and heroines who helped the oppressed escape the Nazi terror, Crown Publishers, New York 1957, 224 pp.
Guenther Weisenborn: *Der lautlose Aufstand. Bericht ueber die Widerstandsbewegung des deutschen Volkes 1933–1945,* Rowohlt, Reinbek 1953, 348 pp.
Annedore Leber: *Conscience in Revolt*. Sixty-four stories of resistance in Germany 1933–1945, Vallentine & Mitchell, London 1957, 270 pp.

Attitude of Allied or Neutral States

Norman Bentwich: *They found refuge*. An account of British Jewry's work for victims of Nazi oppression, The Cresset Press, London 1956, 227 pp.
Carl Ludwig: *Die Fluechtlingspolitik der Schweiz in den Jahren 1933 bis 1945. Bericht an den Bundesrat zuhanden der eidgenoessischen Raete*, no publisher stated, 1957, 416 pp.
Alfred A. Haesler: *Das Boot ist voll. Die Schweiz und die Fluechtlinge 1933–1945*, Fretz & Wasmuth Verlag, Zurich/Stuttgart 1967, 364 pp.
Leni Yahil: *Test of a Democracy*. The rescue of Danish Jewry in World War II, Magnes Press, Jerusalem 1966, 332 pp.

Arthur D. Morse: *While Six Million died*. The untold and shocking account of the apathy shown, and the deliberate obstruction placed by the USA and Britain in the way of attempts to save the Jewish people from Hitler's 'final solution', Secker & Warburg, London 1968, 420 pp.

Trials

Trial of German Major War Criminals before the International Military Tribunal, Nuremberg 1947 (42 vols.)

Bernd Naumann: *Auschwitz. Bericht vom Prozess vor dem Schwurgericht Frankfurt*. Athaeneum, Frankfurt 1965, 552 pp.

Hannah Arendt: *Eichmann in Jerusalem*. Viking Press, New York 1963, 312 pp.

Gideon Hausner: *Justice in Jerusalem*. Nelson, London 1967, 528 pp.

Ralph Giordano/H. G. van Dam: *KZ-Verbrechen vor deutschen Gerichten*. Europaeische Verlagsanstalt Frankfurt a.M.; 1962, Vol. I, 583 pp.; 1966, Vol. II, 514 pp.

Bibliographies

Ilse R. Wolff: *German Jewry, its History, Life and Culture*. The Wiener Library, London 1958

Ilse R. Wolff: *Persecution and Resistance under the Nazis*. The Wiener Library, London 1960

Jacob Robinson/Philip Friedman: *Guide to Jewish History under Nazi Impact*. Bibliographical Series No. 1, Yad Washem and YIVO, New York 1960, 425 pp.

SS Ranks and their Equivalents in the British Army

Unterscharfuehrer—Corporal
Hauptscharfuehrer—Staff Sergeant
Untersturmfuehrer—Second Lieutenant
Obersturmfuehrer—Lieutenant
Hauptsturmfuehrer—Captain
Sturmbannfuehrer—Major
Obersturmbannfuehrer—Lieutenant-Colonel
Brigadefuehrer—Major-General
Gruppenfuehrer—Lieutenant-General
Obergruppenfuehrer—General of Infantry, etc.

Wehrmacht Ranks and their Equivalents in the British Army

Oberleutnant—Lieutenant
Hauptmann—Captain
Generalleutnant—Lieutenant-General
Generaloberst—General

Others

Gauleiter—Chief of Administrative Region of NSDAP
Amtsleiter—Head of Administrative Office of NSDAP
''Der Stuermer''—notoriously virulent anti-Semitic newspaper
Wachtmeister—Sergeant (Police)
Sonderkommandos—Special Squads

223

It was possible to produce this book in the short period of two years because the author was able to take advantage of the preparatory research into the history of the Third *Reich* that has been carried out since the war by several large institutes. They all put the collections in their archives at the disposal of the author and gave him every support in this project. Above all thanks are due to:

Dr. Léon Czertok, Secretary-General, Centre de Documentation Juive Contemporaine, Paris,
Dr. Louis de Jong, Director of the Rijksinstituut voor Oorlogsdocumentatie, Amsterdam,
Prof. Dr. Bernard Mark, former Director of the Zydowski Instytut Historyczny, Warsaw,
Mgr. Kazimierz Smolen, Director of the Panstwowe Muzeum, Auschwitz,
Dr. Hana Volavkova, former Director of the Statni zidovske Museum, Prague,
Dr. Alfred Wiener, former Director of the Wiener Library, London.

Mme. Olga Wormser and Herr Ulrich Hessel, Paris, Herr Dr. Leo Kahn, London, and Herr Dr. A. H. Paape, Amsterdam, Miss Doris Biedermann, Herr Hanno Kremer and Herr Ludwig Thuermer, Berlin, all gave indispensable help in the preparation of this book. The author wishes to express his sincere gratitude to them and to all the other friends and helpers whose names are not mentioned here.

"Dokumenty i Materialy", edited by the Jewish Historical Commission in Poland, was a rich source of hitherto little-known material. The author is indebted to Gerald Reitlinger's *"Die Endloesung"*, and the first two volumes of the collection of documents by Leon Poliakov and Josef Wulf, *"Das Dritte Reich und die Juden"* and *"Das Dritte Reich und seine Diener"* for valuable information and references.

The original German version of *The Yellow Star* was first published in Hamburg in 1960. A number of new photographs, which have come to light since then, and two quotations, which are of particular interest to readers outside Germany, on the conferences of Evian and Bermuda, have been incorporated into the English edition.